THE Influential
Conversationalist

THE Influential Conversationalist

Conversation Skills that Develop Leadership Potential

JEN MUELLER

Print ISBN - 978-0-9893206-0-3
Ebook – 978-0-9893206-1-0

Cover design by Gina O'Daniel, O'Daniel Designs

Cover photo by Tara Gimmer

Printed in the United States of America
Gorham Printing

Talk Sporty to Me
Issaquah, WA
www.TalkSportytoMe.com

*ATTENTION CORPORATIONS, UNIVERSITIES, COLLEGES AND PROFESSIONAL ORGANIZATIONS: Quantity discounts are available on bulk purchases of this book for educational, gift purposes, or as premiums for increasing memberships. Special book covers or book excerpts can be created to fit specific needs. For more information please contact Jen Mueller: Jen@TalkSportytoMe.com

To Layla P.

Grow up to be the rock star
you were meant to be.

PRAISE FOR JEN MUELLER

"A lot of people just want to get the next story or write the next big thing, but Jen actually cares. She's a genuine person in the locker room. There's not too many people in this world who care, so if you've got that you already got my attention. I trust Jen and her approach because she cares."

Bobby Wagner
Seattle Seahawks Linebacker

"Knowing how to talk to people, and more importantly, getting them to talk to you is vital to being a good sideline reporter. I've seen how Jen does this with players and experienced it first-hand being with her on the sidelines. If you want to understand how conversations build relationships, listen to Jen—she's pretty dang good at it."

Erin Andrews
NFL sideline reporter

"Knowing how to receive and convey a message is a skill all good sideline reporters have. Through Jen's many years of experience she has mastered the art of communicating and now is sharing her practical tips for conversation to help make a difference in your career. No matter what your job is, everyone can benefit from being a more confident and effective communicator."

Alex Flanagan
NFL sideline reporter

"Having worked with Jen for more than a decade, I know she can talk. More importantly for us at ROOT SPORTS, she can get athletes to talk about critical moments of their games. It's a skill that translates to everyday life, whether in sports broadcasting or the business world. The ability to communicate opens doors. Take advice from Jen, it's worth it."

Brad Adam
ROOT SPORTS Anchor

"Jen's preparation and knowledge are obvious to anyone who watches or listens to her, but what I noticed the first time I met her and every time since, is the way she is off the air: How she treats people...how she listens...her kindness to everyone who's in her orbit. I respect what Jen does, she's terrific at it, but what I admire is WHO she is. There are so many men and women wanting to do what Jen does and what I would tell them is watch not only what she does....but the WAY she does it. That's a terrific place to start."

Laura Okmin
NFL sideline reporter

"It's a given sidelines reporters talk for a living. Not all of them go out of their way to build relationships like Jen does. Being a great communicator is as much about listening as it is about creating great conversation. Jen is great at that. I've seen her use that skill many times and she's mastered it. It doesn't surprise me she shared her conversation strategies in this book because she wants others to succeed. I benefit from that on the sidelines with her and now you will too in The Influential Conversationalist."

Pam Oliver
NFL sideline reporter

"When people ask me how to get ahead in business, I explain they should get really good at golf—following Jen's instruction would be the next best thing. Sports conversations open doors. Jen's approach is practical, easy-to-follow and a must for becoming a better communicator, positioning yourself for bigger opportunities in your career, and of course becoming an Influential Conversationalist. That, and it is much easier than trying to correct that slice of yours."

Angie Mentink
ROOT SPORTS Anchor

ACKNOWLEDGEMENTS

Writing a book requires dedication on the part of more than the author. There are many people who deserve special thanks, starting with my parents, who laid the foundation for this book years ago. Whining was not tolerated in the house. Excuses were not accepted. What I thought was unfair at the time turned out to be an incredibly valuable mindset and approach throughout my career. In addition, I've never encountered a professional setting more intimidating than a few of the conversations I've had sitting across from my father. His firm, but fair, approach didn't always lead to the outcome I wanted, but I never questioned his wisdom or his love.

I am incredibly grateful to the athletes and coaches I work with. Thank you for allowing me to tell your stories. I owe a special thanks to Doug Baldwin, Richard Sherman, Kam Chancellor, Bobby Wagner, K.J. Wright, Shawn O'Malley, Chris Iannetta, Kyle Seager, Robinson Cano, Nelson Cruz and a handful of scouts for participating in this project. Thank you for your time, professionalism, insights and most of all your friendship. I am incredibly lucky to have you in my corner.

This book wouldn't have been written without the masterful work of my editor Melina. Thank you for using your talents to make me look good.

Lastly, to my husband Paul who endured my writing inspirations at 4am and endless conversations about what I should write. You knew how to tell me what I needed to hear. I should listen to you more often. I love you.

"Commit to the Lord whatever you do and your plans will succeed."

PROVERBS 16:3

CONTENTS

Foreword xiii

Intro: What's Your Excuse? 1

1 **The Influential Conversationalist** 13

The Conversation Crisis 15

2 **Word Problems** 29

What Do I Say? 32

Success Statements 34

3 **What Else Do I Say?** 47

Building Rapport 56

4 **Cheering Versus Rooting** 61

Putting the Fan in "Fanatic" 62

5 **Less Talk, More Action** 71

The Story Behind the Super Bowl Ring 72

No Timetable 78

6 **Be Interesting** 85

Career Development 86

Talk Yourself Into It 88

7 **Does This Make My Bias Look Big?** 101

8 **Sexism Versus Poor Communication Skills** 111

Speak Up 112

9 **What's Left to Say?** 125

The Rest of the Story 132

BONUS **The No-Stress Way to Build Rapport** . . . 135

Bringing It All Together 140

About the Author 143

"I think leadership is first defined by influence. In order to lead, you have to influence people to trust you to lead them. Influence is developed in relationships, and to me, true leadership can only be constructed through relationships and those relationships lead to influence and allow you to lead."

DOUG BALDWIN, JR.
SEATTLE SEAHAWKS RECEIVER

For as long as I've been with the Seattle Seahawks, Jen has been a pleasant personality on our sideline. She's there to do her job as a reporter, but she cares about more than just the game or the next interview.

Jen is quick to share the story about our first interview. She'll tell you it wasn't her best and that I saved her from being embarrassed. I don't know how true that is, but I do know she is intentional about the time she spends talking to me and the rest of the team during the week. She works at building relationships with us and it shows on game day. Her ability to talk to us develops the trust needed to do interviews after games—whether we win or lose. She's able to navigate those conversations with grace and we trust her to ask the right questions at the right time.

Effective communication shows up in a lot of different ways in football. As a wide receiver, I have to be on the same page as the quarterback in order to execute my job at a high level. Our ability to communicate is vital to our success on the field, but it is off the field where we cultivate our relationship and trust through communication.

The conversations you have in your work setting sound different, but the same principles apply. You need to not only talk to the people around you, but be able to communicate effectively. You're not always going to know what to say, and sometimes what you say won't come out right, but if you use the techniques Jen demonstrates in the book you'll be well on your way to communicating more effectively, becoming an Influential Conversationalists and finding new ways to lead.

Doug Baldwin Jr.
Seattle Seahawks Receiver

What's Your Excuse?

The officials never "cost" a team the game.

That's not to say officials don't make bad calls or costly errors in big moments...they do.

But they never cost a team the game.

It's a lesson I first learned as a young athlete courtesy of my father, who never allowed the officials to be scapegoats for our mistakes or lack of execution. Attempting that tact as part of a postgame conversation during the ride home was a non-starter. In fact, I couldn't even finish the sentence before my father would say, "The officials didn't cost you that game Jennifer." End of story.

When I became a high school football official, I understood his statement in a whole new light. When coaches, athletes, parents and fans screamed and blamed the officials for losses, they were yelling at me and the guys I officiated with. I walked off the field several times thinking, "Yeah, I blew that call on second down in the third quarter, but your kid dropped two balls that hit his hands. Your quarterback failed to get rid of the ball and took a sack on third down. Your linebacker missed 6 tackles during the game and your kick coverage had holes big enough for me to run through... and you want to blame *me* for the loss? What kind of fairy tale are you living in?"

Blaming others is so much easier than admitting you lost control of a situation or didn't execute.

It's true in football. It's true in school. It's true in relationships. And it's true in your career.

It's so much easier to blame someone else than admit your actions (or inaction) caused you to be passed over for a promotion. It's hard to imagine you don't get paid the same as someone else because you're not doing as much as they are. It's so much easier to think corporate agendas are holding you back, than to come to grips with the fact you don't want the additional hours and responsibilities required to earn a promotion. It's all a different way of saying, "the official cost the team (or me) the game." It's the same mindset, the same set of excuses.

You control so much more than you think.

When you don't control what you can control, you have no one to blame but yourself. Some of the most successful people I know, ones I work with daily, subscribe to this mantra.

Throughout the course of my career as a sideline reporter, I've conducted thousands of postgame interviews. After tough games or particularly hard losses, I'll often try to offer an athlete an excuse or way to explain the outcome:

> "Did the field conditions play a factor?"
>
> "Did the opposing team run something different than you saw on film study?"
>
> "Did the hit you took earlier in the game affect your ability to run the route?"

They're legitimate questions. They're also softball questions that offer a potentially easy way out. After all, a lack of success could be the result of any number of outside factors.

Except that's not how athletes view it. Elite players don't buy into that line of thinking. Their response usually sounds something like, "That's no excuse. That's not why we lost."

They'll go on to explain the number of things they could have done better to produce a different or more favorable result.

It's one of the things I love about the mindset of an athlete. Of course there are outside factors. Officials miss calls, people get hurt, and playing in subzero temperatures can cause problems...but you know what? The top athletes don't care. In the end, athletes believe if they control what they can control success will follow.

Seattle Seahawks Pro Bowl linebacker Bobby Wagner explains it like this:

> "There's no room for excuses or anything of that nature. I think the best leaders are the ones who not only hold others accountable, but hold themselves accountable. There's no room for excuses because excuses stop things from getting done."

Excuses stop things from getting done.
That statement is true in football and life in general.
You might not even realize you're doing it, because some excuses start off as facts. For example:

Fact: I don't like talking to groups of people.

Excuse: I can't lead a team of people because I'm not good at presenting information to a group.

Fact: I don't have as much time in the organization as two other people on my team.

Excuse: I don't have enough experience to apply for a new job opening because there are people in the organization more qualified than I am to do the job.

Fact: I don't have a business degree.

Excuse: I can't start a business or be on a management team because I haven't taken business classes.

The excuses, not the actual facts, are getting in the way. Just look at those same facts presented differently:

Fact: I don't like talking to groups of people.

What It Actually Means: I would prefer to lead small teams or find a role that allows me to work one-on-one with someone, because I'm not comfortable talking to large groups of people.

Fact: I don't have as much time in the organization as two other people on my team.

What It Actually Means: I don't have much time in this organization, but I do have ample work experience on my resume from my previous jobs, which means I'm qualified to apply for this opportunity.

Fact: I don't have a business degree.

What It Actually Means: I'll bring a different perspective to the business after honing my skills for 20 years in a specific industry.

From here on out, enough of the excuses. Stop waiting for someone else to win the game for you. Take the actions needed to get the win yourself.

That's what this book is about: giving you tools to control what you can control in your career (your qualifications, competency and confidence). Master those things and the promotions, paychecks and opportunities will follow. But beware—so will your irritation at people who want to blame everyone else for their inability to succeed. Personally, I don't have patience for those folks anymore...especially when the solution starts with improved conversation skills.

Do you realize one of the biggest predictors of your success is the ability to communicate? As a sports broadcaster, I've got that in spades. It's a God-given talent in my case, but the skill can be learned by those who weren't born with an innate talent in this area. If you are saying, "Jen, I've tried learning this before and it never works—I still suck at business communication." I have good news—it's not you. Business communication is not taught in an effective way.

How do I know?

The corporate world believes business communication gets taught through books, college classes and corporate training sessions.

Unfortunately, "business communication" is a category of books, a description of a class and a type of training session.

Do you know what it isn't? An actual communication style.

Which means you can read all the books you want (including this one) and take classes, but the only way you're going to master the skill and stop sucking in conversations at work is to:

1. Actually talk to people you work with.

2. Understand people are people.

3. Recognize everyone hears messages and communicates differently.

Learning how to communicate more effectively (or at all, given the communication crisis facing the current generation) is within your control right now and has a tangible impact on your career.

As a sports broadcaster, business owner and an Influential Conversationalist, I'll give you the tools to improve your communication skills. And, I'll provide a conversation process that makes everyday interactions easier, more influential, more productive and get you to the point where they feel like second nature.

You're not going to like everything I have to say, but if you wanted to hear the same old lines, you wouldn't have picked up this book.

I also realize there's a chance you've picked up one of my other books. First, thank you! I am flattered you liked my book(s) enough to pick up another one. Second, if that's the case, you might recognize a few main themes or a paragraph or two might sound familiar, which is completely intentional. No, I'm not delusional in thinking anything I've said has become gospel. However, I do hope at some point the themes start resonating and the encouraged actions take hold. Why?

Because I know they make a difference. Which is why I keep writing and speaking on the topic.

Each chapter was written as a stand-alone module. You can start from the beginning and read straight through as you would with any other book, or you can pick the chapters that apply most to you. If reading an entire chapter (or anything more than 140 characters) seems daunting, you'll be relieved to know each chapter includes a Tweetable summary (or two) of 140 characters or less.

One final note, the athletes quoted in this book are male. The reason for that is simple—these are the players I work with on a regular basis. I have developed relationships and earned their trust. They are the best resources I have at providing perspective and insight on the relationship between sports and leadership. And, they're the ones who can give the most honest feedback on the conversation strategies I outline in the book because they are the ones who see it in practice every day during the season.

I primarily cover men's teams and several of the athletes were gracious enough to help me with this project. Don't read anything else into it. But do understand, my entire career has been spent in the most male-dominated, testosterone-driven environment you could ever imagine: professional sports locker rooms. I have not only succeeded in holding my own, but I've been very successful in my career, covering some of the biggest games in the history of Seattle sports. If you're looking for a real-life approach to succeeding in a male-dominated environment—you've come to the right place. If you just want a different way to look at business communication and leadership—I've got that too. So, let's get started.

Influential Conversationalist Strategy

Excuses get in the way of your success (and quite often the facts). Identify and write down two things you've said recently about your opportunity for success. Examine the statements and be honest in determining if it's a fact or an excuse. Using the examples from this chapter, rewrite any excuse statements as fact statements.

Each of your fact statements should not only highlight your skills, but get you thinking about where you have the most control over your career opportunities. For example, if you want to start a business but don't have a business degree, instead of pointing out your lack of that piece of paper, you'll want to look for ways to leverage your diverse business background when talking to people about your startup.

Sports Watch and Talk

The Sports Watch and Talk is designed to reinforce concepts presented in each chapter and give you different ways to view and approach sports fandom. When you watch sports, it's not just about what you're seeing on the field or court. Athletes deal with the same challenges everyone else faces in their careers. Their high-profile jobs mean they're regularly on TV, radio and social media. That exposure provides entertainment, yes, but it can provide you with so much more. Throughout this book, you'll get suggestions on how to watch games with an eye toward building stronger business relationships and developing better communication skills.

In some cases, you'll be using a sports scenario as a small talk topic that springboards into a bigger business conversation. In other examples, the talking portion of the "Watch and Talk" will be more of an internal conversation. Either way, when you watch sports, use your observations as a reminder of how you want to communicate, approach career challenges, celebrate wins and control what you can control.

One more thing…don't limit yourself to professional sports, televised games or the traditional big four sports of football, basketball, baseball and hockey. A sports event could also be beach volleyball, golf, the Olympics or your child's Little League game. There are different types of sports, but each event and athlete provides examples of conversations that can be useful in business.

With that in mind here's your first Watch and Talk example:

Athletes deal with success and failure in every game and on every play. Watch their reactions to plays with unfavorable results. In baseball, it could be the guy who just struck out on a called third strike. Does he slam his bat and throw his helmet or does he keep his composure and walk back to the dugout? In football, it could be the cornerback who gets called for pass interference. Does his throw his hands up, and run over to the official to plead his case? Or does he walk back to the huddle and get ready for the next play?

Pay attention to how you react to their reactions. Are you frustrated when a player throws up his hands and runs over to complain to the official? Do you yell at the TV and tell him to stop whining? Do you tend to side with the player and think he got robbed?

Think about a recent reaction you had to an unfavorable situation at work. Did you come across like one of the players you were just complaining about during the game? Controlling what you can control includes your emotions as well as the actions you take to influence the situation. Next time you watch a game, take a minute to mentally check in with how you're reacting to situations at work.

Chapter in a Tweet...or Two

"It's easier to blame someone else than admit you failed to get the job done. Control what you can control. That's when you find success."

"Learning how to communicate more effectively is within your control right now and has a tangible impact on your career via @JenTalksSports"

CHAPTER 1

The Influential Conversationalist

How would you identify the most influential person in your office?

Do you think about job titles, seniority or pay scale? Those could be indicators (ones that likely point to someone in an executive role). This is someone who signs the paychecks, sets the direction for the company and puts policies in place.

But what about the person who's got the most influence on your daily routine? Who do you talk with most during the day? Who appears to be "in-the-know" about what's coming down the pike? Whose opinion to do you trust and value? Who seems to have the ear of the decision makers?

The person who fits that description is an Influential Conversationalist and has a hand in much more of the day-to-day goings on than you might realize. An Influential Conversationalist knows how to talk to people in a way that gets stuff done. Not by barking out orders or setting mandates, but by building relationships and communicating effectively.

Influential Conversationalists are the go-to folks when you need feedback, or are looking for a critical eye or valued opinion. They're the ones in the middle of big conversations (ones that are probably above their paygrade) because they're good at talking. They know what to say in the right moments and, perhaps more importantly, know how to say it in an appropriate way.

An Influential Conversationalist can quite literally talk their way into bigger opportunities by mastering one interaction at a time. That's not to say they don't need the skills or the resume to match, but resumes look alike. Conversation skills are a much more valued commodity.

Conversations are the starting point for relationships. Conversations give you a chance to voice your ideas and opinions. A seemingly small conversation handled well can lead to a higher profile conversation and face time with decision makers. (Think, pitching an idea to your manager that's presented so well, she facilitates a meeting with the next level manager who could actually put your idea into motion.)

An Influential Conversationalist knows leadership starts with effective communication skills, so they "show up" differently in daily interactions. They know career advancement means they're gonna have to do some talking. Given the current conversation crisis, this isn't always an easy feat, which is all the more reason to be prepared for opportunities when they present themselves.

The Conversation Crisis

Blame it on our overscheduled lives (leading to growing deadlines and a need for increased efficiency). Or, you can take it a step further and blame it on technology. Regardless of the root cause, it is time to declare ourselves in a conversation crisis. Think I'm being too dramatic? Consider this:

- When was the last time you picked up the phone to *call* and ask a friend to join you for dinner instead of just shooting her a text?

- When was the last time you walked across the room to *talk* to a colleague at his or her desk instead of firing off an email with a meeting request?

- When was the last time you *asked* a stranger to take a picture for you instead of snapping a selfie?

Technology has not only changed our daily routines, but eliminated a lot of reasons to talk to each other during the day. I'm guessing you've joined the online shopping trend to avoid the hassles of dealing with crowds. But in addition to bypassing those crowds, you're also avoiding conversations and interactions with other people.

Small talk and daily interactions have become an inconvenience—a deterrent to checking things off a to-do list. Polite exchanges are avoided altogether. Partly because it's viewed as a waste of time, and partly because it's uncomfortable.

Technology has made it possible to go about our day without engaging in what used to be normal everyday conversations.

There's no longer a need to talk to a cashier or server. Kids don't need to ring a doorbell and ask if a friend can come out and play. And voicemails are practically a thing of the past (because even if you leave one, those uber-efficient, overscheduled recipients are more likely to call—or text!—you back to find out what you said instead of listening anyway). The result is fewer opportunities to practice the art of delivering a concise, informative message.

Technology has reduced the need to have conversations. As a society, we've accepted these advances without realizing the unintended consequences. If you have less conversations you'll fall out of practice, become uncomfortable and stop doing it altogether. Unless of course you're in the age group that grew up with iPads and smart phones, who never had to talk in the first place.

It's not your fault conversations don't come as naturally as they once did. It is, however, your fault if you don't do something about it. Why does it matter? Because like it or not...your career depends on it.

It's painfully evident there's a conversation crisis... so acknowledging that is the easy part. The question is, what are you going to do about it?

Here's my solution: watch and talk sports.

I'm not just saying that because I'm a sports broadcaster, grew up a sports fan and always jump straight to the sports headlines before I get any other daily news.

You should start with sports because the field of play is one of the only places technology doesn't work as an effective form of interpersonal communication. A quarterback isn't going to text the receiver the route he should run. A point guard isn't going to send a direct message with the inbounds play. There are no group emails sent at halftime with adjustments. Communication during a game, match, round or race happens in real time. In fact, I'd be willing to bet athletes converse at work more than most business professionals in a corporate environment because it's tough to win without having actual conversations with their coworkers (i.e. teammates).

Watching sports provides real life examples of what communication looks like. Talking sports allows you to put the skills in practice.

And before you roll your eyes and say something like, "Sports has nothing to do with work." I promise you this: if you take the strategies I've learned talking sports for a living and apply them to any (dare I say, all?) business conversations, you'll be able to talk your way into just about any opportunity you want. Yes, you need the appropriate education or experience level (those are table stakes), but I'm willing to bet you've got those. So, what's missing that caused you to pick up this book?

If you're frustrated your resume isn't attracting employers, or your college degrees don't impress recruiters, or if you think your work speaks for itself...you're missing the part that makes you valuable to your employer—YOU.

It's you.

It's your unique perspective. It's your ability to put it all together. And I can't see *you* on a piece of paper or email. I can see part of what makes you great, but if left to my own imagination or time constraints, all I'm going to see is another applicant (who might be doing more to capture and retain my attention).

You must learn to talk to people.

Here's what having actual conversations allows you to do:

- **Convey a Message Showcasing Your Accomplishments and Displaying Confidence.**
  How is anyone going to know you're a rock star if you don't let your genius show? Being proactive and engaging in conversations not only opens the line of communication, but shows confidence in your own skills and abilities. When you have

a good conversation strategy you don't have to hope someone approaches you to ask for your ideas. It doesn't mean every conversation you have at work needs to be self-promoting. It does mean you need to have a success statement (see Chapter 2) ready for use in daily interactions.

- **Demonstrate Your Buy-In and Engagement Level.** You know you're stoked about the project you're working on, but what about the people around you? Are they aware of your commitment and engagement level? You really don't want an employer, or coworker for that matter, wondering if you're just going through the motions or if you're truly giving your best effort. Promotions and additional opportunities don't often go to the folks just punching a clock and going through the motions. This does not mean you turn into the office cheerleader by overdoing the "rah-rah" conversations. It does mean you should make it a point to have conversations with coworkers in general—and not make it all about work. Engagement levels are evident when coworkers get along and enjoy working together.

- **Reduce Sexism.** A study by McKinsey and Company (highlighted in Chapter 8) found women were more likely to be ignored at meetings, less likely to get challenging assignments and less likely to be consulted for input on big decisions. All of these factors contribute to sexism and the current pay gap in the United States. But all is not lost. I will show you how they can all be lessened with better communication skills.

- **Develop Listening Skills Fostering Emotional Intelligence.** Society's conversation crisis not only impacts the way we talk, but the way we listen. Talking is not spilling your guts on social media. Listening is not downloading a podcast. Face to face interactions give you an opportunity to read body language, pick up on nonverbal cues, and develop an overall awareness of the situation, the person you're talking to, and your role in that space. The more you talk to people the easier it is to identify the nuances in conversations, which often give as much information as the words being said.

- **Increase Leadership Opportunities.** You can't lead if you're not paying attention to the people around you. Effective leadership requires self-awareness and emotional intelligence. That self-awareness can lead you to identify new opportunities, figure out how your skill set can solve a current problem, or just work as a leader should with the people around him or her. However you look at it, you have to put yourself out there—which is as easy as having daily conversations with people in your office—before someone is going to identify your potential in a leadership position. Sitting at your desk, keeping your head down and hoping someone notices your efforts doesn't work as a career development strategy.

For all these reasons, you should stop minimizing the need for actual conversations in business. Knowing there's a need is one thing. Being able to do something about it is another. We'll dive into each of those bullet points throughout the book.

The first step, for now, is honing your observation skills. We don't want to make any changes to the way you're already interacting with people until you look at those conversations with a critical eye and know 1) whom you're talking to, 2) why you're taking to them and 3) what you're trying to say. We also need to explore the reaction those conversations get. Your observations are going to provide a baseline and a starting point for becoming an Influential Conversationalist.

Talking to people and knowing how to make your message land so it spurs action is effective communication whether you're in a corporate environment or any other business setting.

Critical Conversation Observations:

Since my business setting is a locker room, let's take a look at the way I approach interviews with athletes and how that applies to your conversations at work. While the subject matter differs, I assure you the framework of the conversations is the same.

Who Am I Talking To?

This isn't just a fill-in-the-blank answer with the name of an athlete. When I think about this question in terms of a postgame interview, I'm also thinking about the athlete's personality type, communication style, and comfort level in doing interviews in the first place.

In a corporate setting, you might also want to consider the position of the person you're talking to in relation to your position in the company. For example, are you talking to a manager, a colleague, or an executive?

Why Am I Talking to That Person?

When it comes to postgame interviews, I usually target someone who made a specific play or a stellar overall contribution in the game. Naturally I'm going to want to ask about those particular instances, but I might also be looking for perspective on the team in general, or perhaps insight on a specific teammate. This means in addition to my immediate need for a particular interview, I've got a big-picture goal in mind as well.

There are dozens of reasons you could be having a conversation at work. Perhaps you are just being nice to the person sitting next to you. Or maybe you have a question about a project, need clarification on an email, have an idea you want to share, are inviting someone to lunch, requesting next steps following a performance review...the list goes on and on.

There are three categories of conversations: relationship building, work related, and on the radar. Before you read about each one in detail, take a second and identify the last three conversations you've had. Can you identify which category each one falls into?

You should have conversations in each of these categories on a weekly basis. The *work related* ones are easy and the most natural because they involve the actual work at hand. Those are the conversations about upcoming projects, company goals, or questions about an expense report. In other words, those conversations help you do what you do.

The *relationship building* conversations are the ones that seem like throw away conversations. But don't be fooled! Small talk and polite chitchat while standing in line for coffee are how relationships start. They allow you to build trust and rapport with colleagues and ultimately help you do what you do. I strategically plan these types of conversations with the athletes and coaches I work with. You should too.

On the radar conversations describe your efforts to be seen by key influencers and decision makers. It can be as simple as striking up a conversation about a big game with the CEO while you're both in the elevator or saying "Hi" to your manager in the morning instead of waiting to be noticed at your desk. The purpose of these conversations is to be visible. They give people a reason to not only remember your name, but have a positive association with you. Because at the end of the day, likeability really is the first step in additional opportunities at work.

What Am I Trying to Communicate?

During a postgame interview, I need to do two things: 1) get a player to talk to me and 2) get the player to say something that benefits the audience.

Getting someone to talk is the easy part. Asking the right questions in the right order is more challenging. That's because it requires me to combine what I know from the first two critical observation questions (Who am I talking to? Why am I talking to that person?), and it means I can't ask the same question to every single player and expect to get a good answer. Some athletes enjoy letting their personality show on camera, others are more introverted and shy away from the limelight. An athlete with a dry sense of humor isn't going to respond in the same way as someone who is boisterous and outgoing. A rookie isn't going to have the same perspective as a 10-year veteran. And someone who doesn't speak English as a first language is going to benefit from an approach that accounts for their comfort level in speaking a foreign language.

Diversity in a sports locker room can be more apparent than a traditional corporate setting, but the people you work with have diverse interests, personalities and communication styles too. Similar to my experiences, if you try to have the exact same conversation with every person in your office, you'll fail at communicating. (And be seen as disingenuous, which can be worse than not being noticed at all.)

Think about the conversations you choose to have with one person versus another. For example, when you're planning a trip or a vacation, is there a colleague who loves to travel you always go to for trip advice? Or perhaps there's a foodie in your group who gives the best restaurant or recipe recommendations. And certainly, there's the office jokester who loves to have a good laugh and doesn't appear to take anything too seriously.

Do you talk to all those folks the same way? Probably not. Are you that particular, thoughtful, or strategic when it comes to a business conversation? You should be.

What you're trying to communicate is important, but if you don't talk in a way your colleagues or clients want to hear, you're minimizing the chance your message will be heard and acted on. For the record, this doesn't mean you avoid the tough questions or you refrain from bringing up a difficult topic that needs to be addressed. It means you're cognizant of your colleagues' communication styles, your objective, and the environment you're in.

....

You cannot apply a one size fits all
approach to conversations and think you're
excelling at business communication.

....

There is no homogenous way to approach business communication that works across the board with everyone to foster buy-in and increase productivity. You can't deliver your message the same way to everyone and think it's going to resonate equally. To really have a message hit home in day-to-day interactions you've got to have a personalized approach.

The only way to develop that kind of approach is to have actual, real life conversations. Plural. Start talking to people. Get a feel for their personalities and communication styles. Talk about things outside of work (I always recommend sports) to build rapport. That's how business gets done and it's what *business communication* really is.

If you'd like more examples of how conversation approaches succeed or fail, start using a critical eye to observe not just your own interactions, but the ones that happen before and after sporting events. An athlete's body language, facial features and actual response can give you an indication of the effectiveness of that approach.

Influential Conversationalist Strategy

Be purposeful in having conversations and take steps to increase your overall awareness of those interactions. Spend a few minutes considering a handful of your recent interactions...

What kind of critical observations can you make?

Which conversations make you most nervous?

Which ones do you go out of your way to avoid?

What's one objective for you in becoming a better conversationalist?

Sports Watch and Talk

Spend five minutes watching a game or sporting event. Pay attention to how many conversations or one-on-one interactions take place during that time. You'll probably notice none of the conversations are particularly long. There simply isn't time during the middle of an event. You'll also notice there's a different intent behind each interaction and even though they are short, a lot gets done. Here are a few examples of what you might see:

- A player congratulating a teammate
- A coach talking to an official for clarification on a call
- A manager calling down to the bullpen for a reliever

- A quarterback barking out directions at the line of scrimmage
- A coach calling a timeout to get everyone on the same page
- A player bantering with an opponent because they used to be teammates
- A golfer talking strategy with the caddy
- A swimmer getting a last-minute pep talk from a coach

You could be having the same kinds of conversations with the people you work with. In fact, you should be having similar conversations. This week, engage in three conversations (not via text, email or social media, but actual conversations) using one or more of the examples you saw in a sporting event. If face to face interactions aren't comfortable for you, remember these aren't long drawn out monologues. These interactions can be as short as saying, "Great job in that meeting!" to a colleague or asking a manager for clarification on an email you received.

Chapter in a Tweet...or Two

"Sitting at your desk and hoping someone notices your efforts doesn't work as a career development strategy. Talking does. @JenTalksSports"

"Understand how to make your message land in a way that leads to action. That's effective communication in any business setting."

CHAPTER 2

Word Problems

Math baffles me. It was always a source of angst in school (and resulted in the lowest grade on my report card). Simple math is fine, but start throwing letters into the mix and I'm confused. I remember shortly after starting algebra, my father spent an entire evening at the dining room table with me and a bowl of fruit doing his best to explain how $2x + b = 15$. I appreciated the visuals, but the fruit only added to the confusion. (So, grape times 4 equals banana?) I struggled all the way through calculus, marveling at how it could make sense to my father and many of my classmates, but never to me.

The tables turned in English, persuasive speaking and drama. Anything dealing with the so-called "soft-skills" made perfect sense to me, while the apparent randomness of what made a paper good or argument persuasive frustrated my analytically-minded friends. What they didn't see were the strategic possibilities and the process used to develop effective exchanges. It's not random.

I didn't see algebra as the problem-solving tool it is. I do, however, see the problem-solving potential in every conversation. We could even call them "word problems" to keep the mathematical theme.

A conversation has a beginning, middle and end just like a math problem. The better you are at executing each step of the process, the greater your chances of becoming a good conversationalist and an effective communicator. This carries more weight than the accomplishments on a resume, or a baseball card in the case of Seattle Mariners third baseman, Kyle Seager.

"Everybody who gets to this level, or the professional level, has God-given talent or ability," Seager explained. "For me personally, it's the guys who can communicate and talk, who can not only express themselves, but who can listen and learn the most. They potentially help themselves the most."

"Communication is a major key in football," agrees Seattle Seahawks linebacker K.J. Wright. "Communication is a major key in life. It's very important to understand what other guys are thinking so you can all be on the same page. You don't want to be on one page and the buddy beside you be on a completely different page."

Their points are well taken by the person who got "talks too much" on every report card. (That was me, in case you were wondering.) However, conversations

aren't just about talking. There's also a listening compo-
nent, and an element of critical thinking.

If you can't get people to talk to you, you're not just
missing an opportunity to connect with them. You're
missing a chance to grow and learn.

This doesn't mean every conversation should be a
drawn out exchange. Conversations vary, and each one
can be as short (or as long) as needed. Athletes, for example, can communicate a massive amount of information in a single word or phrase. Don't try to force
more words into your interactions. Instead look at your
overall approach.

A quote attributed to Mark Twain (and many others
have made similar statements) comes to mind when
thinking of this concept, "Forgive me, if I had more
time, I would have written a shorter letter." Being com-
pelling and concise takes work. Even great wordsmiths
struggle with this from time to time. It is easy to ramble
on quickly, but getting to the point in the way someone
wants (or needs to hear it) takes effort.

---

*The Influential Conversationalist has the confidence
to make an introduction, possesses the skills to
make a positive impression and ability to guide a
conversation from beginning, middle and end.*

Make it easy for people to talk to you and you'll find
it easy to connect with them. As long as you know what
to say.

What Do I Say?

I get that question a lot. "What do I say?" seems to have surpassed, "What's it like in a locker room?" and "Are the guys really naked?" as the question I get asked the most these days. (In case I made you curious, I would say "it depends" and "sometimes" as the answers to those two questions.)

The question at hand is usually fueled by the desire to make a good first impression, and often asked while assuming everyone else is better at making an introduction. Not true. Consider a conversation I took part in earlier this year that started with a familiar sounding question.

"What do you say when you meet a famous or very influential person?" a friend asked. This friend happens to be a college professor who was in Seattle as part of a guys' weekend. "We talked about this a couple times today," he explained. "We've all been fortunate to meet some very influential people during the course of our careers, but the more we talk about it the more we realize we might have blown those interactions and looked ridiculous. What should we have said?"

"It depends on what you were trying to get out of the conversation," I responded as the wheels in my head started turning. I found it curious these highly successful, well established professionals who, by all accounts, communicate effectively, were asking this question.

Everyone struggles with communication anxiety from time to time—even very skilled conversationalists.

What does that mean for you? There could be a whole lot of folks who don't know how to start a conversation with you (even people who you think should be good at this). People around you might be wondering what to say after you introduce yourself.

Think about that. If you're waiting for someone else to take charge and lead the conversation you could be waiting a while. If you assume everyone is better at this than you, or finds it easier than you do, you're not giving yourself enough credit. More importantly, you could be missing out on important connections and conversations.

My friend and his buddies posed three different scenarios and asked how I would respond to meeting influential people in these situations:

1. What do you say if you find yourself in an elevator with the CEO of the company?

2. What do you say when meeting a potential business connection for the first time?

3. What do you say if you meet a famous person?

Think of these scenarios as the "known" in a math equation. The challenge you're trying to solve is the given and addresses the beginning of the exchange. It's up to you to figure out the middle and the end of the conversation...without turning into a weirdo super-fan who gushes something like, "Oh my gosh, oh my gosh.

I can't believe I ran into you. This is crazy. Is this real? Pinch me. I can't believe my luck in meeting you!"

As someone trying to become more influential, any variation of that response should be avoided, unless you're trying to become the benchmark for crazy super-fan reactions.

Assuming you'd like to have a successful business exchange, or pleasant conversation, you need a way to address the beginning, middle and end of a conversation concisely. You need a success statement.

Success Statements

Each scenario mentioned has a different objective, but all involve a success statement which touches on either their success or yours. A success statement does three things:

- makes an introduction and a positive first impression

- provides a way to highlight your accomplishment

- connects what you're doing to their overall objective

It also exploits a conversation loophole.

You know that moment when someone says to you in passing, "How's it going?" or "How are you today?"

You're expected to say something along the lines of, "Fine." or "Good." If you really want to seem friendly you'll say, "I'm well thanks! How are you?" But what do we really get out of that exchange? Outside of general pleasantries and following the social norm, there's not much information exchanged. I'm not saying you shouldn't be willing to say, "Hi." I'm suggesting you make that exchange more useful.

Here's an example. You're walking down the hall as all the department heads are leaving their weekly managers' meeting. One of them spots you and says, "Good morning! How's it going today?" Instead of a predictable one word response, what if you said something like this:

> "I'm great! I just landed a new client after almost a year of conversations. I'm sending over the final proposal later this morning."

That kind of response allows you to answer the question, while offering insight on your recent success. There is a beginning, middle and end, with an option for follow up. Let's break it down:

- I'm great! (beginning)

- I just landed a new client after almost a year of conversations. (middle)

- I'm sending over the final proposal later this morning. (end)

This statement puts a nice little bow on the step you're taking as a result of your success. That can be the end of the conversation, or just the start if it piqued the interest of the manager who wants to hear more and asks follow up questions.

Here's why success statements are so important: no one is (or ever will be) as invested in your success as you are. The people in your office aren't keeping track of your wins like you do. Your contributions are important, and so is your ability to spotlight them, especially to decision makers, managers and members of the leadership team. You need to have a way to highlight your success, and engage in a conversation that reflects positively on you.

And, whatever you do, please do not say you are "busy." If you have said this before, don't beat yourself up (we all have). It is a very common response in the workplace—and might seem like people would think you are working hard when you respond this way. Sadly, you would be mistaken.

Let's look at that managers' meeting example again: all the department heads are leaving their weekly meeting and one of them says, "Good morning! How's it going today?" To which you respond, "Whoa man, we are crazy busy down here—work, work, work!" as you speed away from the conversation.

There are two ways to infer this statement 1) you are too busy to take on more work and might not be doing your job efficiently, and/or 2) you are oblivious to the workloads of others (read: everyone is busy). Are you busier than those direct managers or the CEO? They might think you are implying you are, which can be insulting. In any case, the result will likely be people not asking how you are anymore and not thinking of you for upcoming tasks ("No, let's not give her this project, she is way too busy and couldn't handle it.")

Every conversation you have either reinforces what people think about you or gives them a chance to rethink what they know.

What are you telling people with a one word answer?

How much more could you tell them in two or three sentences?

What if the only interaction you have with a high level manager, or the CEO of the company, occurs in passing or in an elevator?

Be ready to make the most of that exchange.

Which brings us back to the question posed by my friend, "What do you say if you find yourself in an elevator with the CEO of the company?" Here's what you need:

1. A way to break the ice

2. A recent success to highlight

3. A concise delivery

Breaking the ice is easy. You could go with a standard, "How are you?" or "How was your weekend?" Social norms work in your favor when the CEO gives a short answer like, "I'm pretty good." and turns the question back to you by saying, "How are you?" When the ball is in your court, you offer a pleasantry and highlight one recent success, like I did in this statement:

> "I'm great, especially after earning an Emmy for a show I did on Ken Griffey Jr's Hall of Fame Induction. Now I've got to try and do it again."

I use this tactic a lot, especially with front office executives of the teams I cover or when I know the president of the organization will be attending a staff meeting or making a trip to our office building. I know he's aware of my general contributions. I want to make sure he's aware of specific ways I'm working to make the company better. I want a statement that reflects well on me and the organization.

Your success statement needs to be conversational, topical and easy to remember. It's not a canned elevator pitch. This is part of the ongoing dialogue showcasing the rock star you are.

In developing your own success statements, consider the audience and your professional goals. If you have face time with the CEO, even if it's just 60 seconds in an elevator, do you really want to talk about how you've avoided eating dessert for three straight nights and gone to the gym for three straight days? While that's an accomplishment (and a success in my book) it's not going to do anything to advance your career. Think about what matters to a CEO or any leader in the company. They're interested in productivity, results, deadlines, budgets and revenue. Make sure your success highlights something that not only reflects positively on you, but what you're doing to impact the overall health or success of the company.

Because that is always on the mind of a company leader, you don't have to belabor the point in your short interaction. In fact, it's better you keep the exchange brief. This isn't part of a performance review, it's not a one-on-one meeting, it's a small talk conversation in an elevator. If the CEO is curious, they'll ask for more information. If they don't continue the conversation, you can still feel good about how you took advantage of the opportunity, and the message you conveyed. In addition, you did it in a natural way. You don't have to force the conversation. It's not bragging and it's not begging for attention.

The same techniques apply when you're meeting a potential business connection for the first time. You want to be able to break the ice, make the introduction and highlight a success that would interest them. It's the approach I used the first time I spoke with NFL Commissioner Roger Goodell. (In case you aren't familiar with the hierarchy, this is kind of a big deal—if football was a country, he would be the king.) The conversation went like this:

> "Hi Roger, my name is Jen Mueller and I'm the sideline reporter for the Seahawks. I know you're focused on the female fanbase. I'm doing my part by speaking at women's conferences in the Northwest on the value of being a football fan in business."

I formulated this conversation with a very specific goal in mind. I wanted to work with the NFL on a large scale. I knew the NFL had identified a desire to grow the female fanbase. I needed to highlight my skills, content and approach in a way that showed value to the NFL's goals. I knew I had a limited amount of time to get the commissioner's attention. He was either going to be interested in what I had to say, or not. He did not have time to waste and I did not have more than 15 seconds to make a good impression.

Delivering my success statement led him to stop, ask more questions and engage in a conversation that provided follow up opportunities. (Awesome.) The commissioner has seen me several times since then. (Double awesome.) Every time he sees me he asks what I'm working on and how the business is going. (Amazing!) The NFL hasn't picked up on my approach yet, but it's never a bad thing to build rapport with the NFL commissioner.

Business connections don't happen overnight, what you're looking for is an approach that gets you a follow up, either in the form of a question that continues the conversation or an actual meeting. A well delivered and properly thought out success statement can do both. Which means you shouldn't try to wing it. You need to have a success statement prepared before you actually need it, because the truth is you don't know when you're going to need it. For example, I had thought about and practiced what I would say if I ever met Roger Goodell for three months before it actually happened.

You don't know when you're going to get into an elevator with a CEO. You don't know who you're going meet at a networking function or sporting event. You should know how to articulate what you're good at and be able to show why your skillset is valuable.

There's one exception to that—when you meet a famous person (the last scenario posed by the college professor). In that case focus on their success, not yours, because the objective for that interaction is probably very different.

My friends were specifically asking about running into movie stars and big-name athletes, but a famous person could also be the CEO of a Fortune 50 company, a multi-billion dollar entrepreneur, or the head coach of an NFL team.

Each year during the NFL Combine, it feels like every

bar and restaurant in Indianapolis turns into a "Who's Who" in football: with coaches, front office personnel and support staff mingling over dinner and drinks.

The Combine also attracts job seekers, like students looking to break into the industry. I was facilitating a career conference for a group of these students and was offering suggestions on how to approach some of their networking conversations. One of the attendees took the mic and asked, "What do I say if I run into Bill Belichick at the bar?"

While it's unlikely, even in this situation to run into New England Patriots' head coach Bill Belichick, it wasn't completely out of the realm of possibility. Which is why I offered the best advice I could think of.

"You don't say anything outside of 'Congratulations on winning the Super Bowl,'" I told the student. "Bill Belichick is not going to be the one to give you a job. He's not the person making entry level hires. If your objective is to get a job, there are better people in the organization to get in front of."

There are two things to consider in this scenario: 1) the overall objective and 2) the relation to the other person in the conversation. If the objective is to get an entry level job, the goal should be to identify the person who posts openings, conducts interviews or hires for that job. That's the person who has the most influence over your success.

Just because a person is famous, or the top decision maker in a company, doesn't mean they are the person who's going to make a decision about you.

Oh, and if you think, "It doesn't hurt to ask." Think again. Similar to the "busy" example above, asking this question shows you don't understand the situation, or your position in the conversation. Remember, every conversation says more about you than just the words you're saying. Restraint is a big part of knowing what to say in those moments. The gushing super-fan isn't great at it, neither is the person who tries to accelerate a business connection in one conversation.

The Influential Conversationalist doesn't worry about the timing of a business relationship. He or she knows how to initiate a productive conversation, solve the "word problem" and highlight their success.

Influential Conversationalist Strategy

Success statements are an important strategy for making the most of limited interactions around key influencers, decision makers and new business contacts. They're also a way for you to take credit for your work without bragging. Remember you're more invested in your success than everyone else, and even though they try to understand or see what you do, it doesn't hurt to remind them from time to time.

For all these reasons, you should have a success statement ready and be able to work it into conversations seamlessly. You'll need a way to make an introduction, highlight a recent success, make a connection between what you do and their needs—and deliver all of this in just two or three sentences.

Here are a few things to consider:

1. If you can't finish the statement in the time it takes to go from one floor on the elevator to the next—it's too long. No exceptions. (Seriously.)

2. Know what constitutes a success. It's not just getting a raise, promotion or award. A success could be streamlining a process, getting a new team member up to speed, reducing the length of weekly meetings, or implementing a new policy. Countless things make you successful. Be able to identify one that resonates most with your audience (i.e. the person you're talking to.)

3. Success statements can be different for different people. For example, when speaking with your direct manager, you might want to highlight a specific project you've completed. But if speaking to a higher level supervisor who isn't plugged in to your day-to-day responsibilities, it might make more sense to mention an award you won last quarter.

Task

Take five minutes to identify one career goal and two recent successes that are stepping stones to reaching that goal. Write out two success statements that allow you to make an introduction, showcase your skills and make a connection with the person you're talking to. Read those scripts out loud. It should sound natural and be easy to remember. You don't want to sound forced or like you're reading a memorized script. Use a success statement three times in the next week when someone asks, "How are you?"

Sports Watch and Talk

Success statements come across in different ways and different situations. A player might say something like this during a postgame interview:

> "We knew all week it was going to be tough to get to the quarterback. When I recognized what I had seen on tape, I knew I could beat him on the edge and get that sack.

This is one way of delivering a success statement, by acknowledging his role in a successful or critical play. I've found athletes are more willing than most to highlight their success because it's hard to argue with the stat sheet. It's not bragging to talk about a great play they made on the ball that resulted in the interception return for a touchdown. It's presenting a statement in relation to the work and preparation they put in.

As you listen to postgame interviews, keep an ear out for different ways success statements are presented.

Then consider using a sports story as a jumping off point for your own success statement. You don't have to wait for someone to ask what you've done at work lately. Piggyback on someone getting credit in the sports world. For example:

> "Nice win last night for the Astros. They're at six straight wins. I feel like I'm almost as locked in as they are with the amount of writing I've finished in the last week."

Chapter in a Tweet...or Two

"Every conversation reinforces what people think about you or gives them a chance to rethink what they know. Make the most of every convo."

"Success statements give you the opportunity to make a positive impression, highlight your skillset and make a business connection."

CHAPTER 3

What Else Do I Say?

A well delivered success statement can get the conversation going, but what happens once you're actually in the conversation? An Influential Conversationalist knows how to read the situation, put people at ease, get everyone on the same page and direct the conversation where it needs to go.

It's a matter of self-awareness. Being able to exercise discernment and practice diplomacy in your conversations. Yes, you need to have direct, pointed or difficult conversations, but those happen *with*, not *at the expense of* the person you're talking to. It's being mindful of how others relate to your conversation objective.

Win or lose, my conversation objective following a game is to get a player to talk to me about that game (in language suitable for a live radio or television audience.) As you can imagine, it's much easier when the team is celebrating a big win and much more challenging after a loss.

Fans who haven't been in a locker room in those

situations often suggest I should act the same whether the team wins or loses. From their point of view, I shouldn't show sympathy, lower my voice or talk to players any differently after a poor outcome. The idea has merit…if I was working with robots instead of human beings with real feelings, who feel terrible about a bad day at work.

It's exactly what I tried to explain to the group of young interns standing outside the Seattle Seahawks locker room following a gut-wrenching loss to the New England Patriots in Super Bowl 49. The interns were excited to be part of the inner circle who got to experience a professional locker room in person. In between their anxious laughs and excited chatter, I suggested they tone it down because their approach was not going to go over well once they got inside. I could see the looks on their faces and could almost hear them calling me a buzzkill…accusing me of ruining their big moment. Except their big moment was coming on the heels of one of the most difficult losses in franchise history.

Those interns were minutes away from being face to face with players who watched their chance to win a second straight Super Bowl evaporate following an interception on the goal line with 26 seconds left in the game. It was one of the most difficult postgame locker rooms I've ever experienced. The players were crushed, heartbroken, angry, frustrated. They were not in the mood for giggly, smiling interns who were oblivious to their pain.

Losing the Super Bowl, or any playoff game, in the final seconds is at the extreme of the emotions I encounter in the locker room. The outcome doesn't change the fact that I have a job to do, but it does determine how I approach that job.

"When it comes to you, you are definitely humble in your approach with us," Seahawks linebacker K.J. Wright said of my demeanor in the locker room. "You understand what kind of mood we're in, and how to approach us. I can see the sympathy on your face when you know, I gotta be careful with K.J. because if I don't he'll get upset and rip me apart. You definitely listen to guys when they talk to you. I definitely appreciate those things about you."

"I would say the best thing you do is, you ask us the right way," Seattle Mariners second baseman Robinson Cano said. "Because sometimes people focus more on what you did wrong compared to asking about the situation, or asking if you can explain it. I've been in big cities and you get people who they don't even think about what they're going to ask in those interviews. They ask whatever they think in the moment."

I wouldn't get the same results if I plowed ahead with my agenda and didn't consider how the other person is receiving the information or the general context of the situation.

As you engage in conversations with colleagues, keep these tips in mind to increase your self-awareness:

Start with the Same Point of Reference. You know why you're talking about a specific topic or asking a specific question, but that doesn't mean the person you're talking to is following the same line of thought. With TV and radio interviews, my words are carefully chosen because time is valuable. I need to make sure I'm on the same page as the athlete I am speaking to, so I often reference a specific play or critical moment during an interview. Sometimes I'll bring up a recent conversation to jog their memory. For example, I might say, "Just yesterday you and I talked about the extra work you've put in on your swing. How did that work pay off in the at bat we saw in the 7th inning?"

Adding a little extra context gives the player an indication of where I'm coming from and where I'd like him to go with the conversation. If I had said, "Tell me about the 7th inning." He could have talked about the routine play he made in the top of the inning, the pitching change two batters before he stepped to the plate, the fans doing "The Wave" or any number of things outside of what I really wanted him to talk about, which was his swing and at bat during a big moment in the 7th inning.

This doesn't just come up during a postgame interview. It happens all the time in business interactions. We give people an awful lot of credit for being able to read our minds. We know what we're talking about, but forget to give our conversation partner a hint as to what that is. As a result, they're confused and might offer a response that doesn't lead to the outcome we expected. Before getting angry or thinking, "Ugh, how is she so dense? That wasn't what I was talking about at all!" consider what you did (and didn't) say in your setup. Provide enough clarity so everyone is starting with the same point of reference.

Avoid Stupid Questions. You know the adage "There are no stupid questions, only stupid answers?" Let's be clear about this: there are stupid questions. Lots of 'em. They can show up in conversations when well-intentioned people try to get to know someone without thinking through the situation. Consider those ridiculous ice-breaker questions like:

"What superpower would you want to possess?"

"If you were stuck on a deserted island with only three things, what would they be?"

"If you were a vegetable which one would you be?"

"What is your spirit animal?"

To be fair, if you're at an event and you're expecting to do a silly ice-breaker activity those questions are fine. (They're still stupid, but at least they're being asked in the right context.) If I'm not expecting these types of questions (and who is when they show up to work?) I'm not going to give you a fun answer that helps you get to know me. I'm not going to have an answer at all. I'm also going to avoid having any additional conversations with you because it's just weird to be asked what kind of tree I would be and why. If people start avoiding you, your visibility and influence decrease.

In addition to skipping the goofy ice-breaker questions, it's best to avoid the "gotcha" questions too, unless you're a detective in a cop show trying to get a confession out of the bad guy.

Is There a Better Way to Say It? Early in my days as a reporter I was sent to get a postgame reaction from inside the clubhouse following a loss. The team lost, in part, to a home run that sailed over the left field fence. The player in left field that day was transitioning from an infield position to the outfield and this was his first start there. In an effort to find a silver lining, and knowing making a play at the wall can be difficult even for experienced outfielders, I asked if there was some relief in knowing he didn't have to make a play on that particular ball since it was a home run.

Seconds after the question was answered with a tepid (but polite) response, a colleague whispered in my ear, "Do you realize the pitcher who gave up that home run is the next locker and heard that question? There was probably a better way to ask the question." My face turned bright red. Of course, there was a better way to ask the question. I had only considered one perspective and failed to think about how someone else involved in the same situation would feel.

This kind of awkward exchange happens when you're either not aware of your surroundings or not paying attention to the other people involved. Both create problems in postgame interviews and business settings alike.

When a majority of your communication takes place in the vacuum of text messages or emails, it's easy to overlook the way your message is received by all parties. An email is sent for a specific reason to a specific person. You don't have to consider anyone else in that exchange. It's a much different story when you're communicating with, in, or near a group. Those interactions require a little nuance and the ability to read the situation and people involved.

Full disclosure: you should always consider the "ripples" created by anything you write or say and think of how you would feel if someone other the intended party heard or read it. Have you ever been looped into an email exchange with a long back and forth and had the opportunity to read everything discussed before you entered the conversation? My advice is to always keep your communication (verbal, email, whatever) at a level you would be happy with anyone being looped in on. You never know who will get CC'd (or who is BCC'd) on an email chain.

Say It Out Loud. "I promise, I'm not crazy. I'm practicing." I explained to the cute guy at the front of the room. He and I were volunteering at the same event. Yes, I was hoping to catch his eye as well...then saw that I had...

but in the wrong way. He was watching me worriedly as I paced the room talking to myself. When I went over to say, "Hi" (an Influential Conversationalist has the confidence to start a conversation, right?) I explained I was the emcee for the event and I was rehearsing my scripts. He must have bought it, because that cute guy at the front of the room is now my husband.

I talk to myself a lot. It's one of the ways I memorize scripts and rehearse. I'm also saying words out loud to make sure they sound the same in real life as they did in my head or on my list of questions.

There are many times where I have to adjust my scripts because the phrasing looks great on paper, but doesn't sound right when said out loud, or is too difficult to say correctly. Think: "spectacular, sunny Sunday" or "shoulder surgery." Both phrases are descriptive and accurate on paper, but don't exactly roll off the tongue during a live broadcast. There's a pretty good chance I'm going to end up slurring those words or getting tripped up when I say them out loud.

The "say it out loud" test not only helps me identify stumble-inducing words, but it provides clarity on whether or not I should ask specific questions. If I put myself in the position of an athlete having to answer the question and I can't come up with a good answer or find myself frowning at the question, I know it's not going to go over well with the player. That doesn't mean I don't ask the tough questions, it means I don't ask "No shit, Sherlock" questions like "How does it feel to win a championship?" (How do you think it feels?) I spend a lot of time trying to understand how the person I'm talking to might respond or react to specific questions and conversations.

The "say it out loud" approach in business helps you experience a conversation ahead of time, allowing you to be more confident when you say the words for real. You can also adjust your message ahead of time if the words you say don't sound like the words you meant.

Don't Watch the Clock. Or your phone or anything else that takes your attention away from the person you're speaking with. If you've taken the time to initiate a conversation and deliver a well-crafted success statement, you need to give the other person (or people) time to react, respond and actually engage in the conversation. If you don't give people the leeway to talk, then you weren't actually trying to communicate, you were trying to dictate.

If you have a deadline or a timeline express it up front, and consider it before starting a conversation. Also, understand you've got to invest uninterrupted time and your undivided attention to form these important connections. I know you've got a lot to do in your day, but so does everyone else. If they took the time to listen to you, return the favor. Otherwise the conversation you intended to use to build a business relationship will end up alienating you in the end.

Building Rapport

When you start applying these techniques to your conversations at work, you'll improve overall communication and develop a rapport that allows you to make mistakes. You're not going to get conversations right every single time. You're going to mess up. You're going to ask a question that didn't come out quite right or make a statement that could be taken the wrong way. That doesn't lessen your status as an Influential Conversationalist, it makes you human.

You're not going to be able to avoid saying something wrong on occasion—but you can lessen the impact by having relationships where people assume the best instead of the worst.

Developing and maintaining good relationships with athletes means if I ask a stupid question, they're not going to point it out during the interview. They'll answer the question as if it was the best thing in the world I could have said. Then, after the interview, we'll laugh about it. Once after a Seahawks preseason game, I asked wide receiver Doug Baldwin, who was a rookie at the time, a question so bad I can't remember what I asked (or, honestly, if my long ramble actually included a question). Doug could have, and maybe even should have, asked me to repeat the question. Instead, he came up with a fantastic answer and helped me save face. That doesn't happen without a level of trust and respect.

When relationships are bad or nonexistent, an athlete would look for ways to make a reporter look bad at every turn. Answers would be terse, combative, and short.

You run into these types of reactions in the corporate world too. Developing good rapport means you worry less about someone trying to find a reason to be mad at you, or parsing every word you say looking for a way to criticize you. It means people aren't looking for a way to bury you in a conversation and make you look bad. When you've invested time in getting to know people, they'll invest good faith back in you.

And, according to a pair of baseball All Stars, they'll be willing to work with you regardless of their personal feelings for you. "Not everyone is going to like you, but if you're trying to get along with everyone, that's something that can lead to good chemistry inside the clubhouse." Robinson Cano said.

"It makes a difference if you talk to each other," said Mariners designated hitter Nelson Cruz, "It gives you a confidence when you need help, or you see something wrong. You can go up to them with respect and let them know what happened and they will listen better. They know when you do talk to them about a mistake you want to benefit them or the team."

Influential Conversationalist Strategy

When building relationships and rapport, utilize a topic that's already top of mind, like sports. Asking a random question, or one that seems to come out of left field will come off sounding stupid and increases the likelihood you're not starting with the same point of reference. It also raises the odds you're in for an awkward exchange and overall communication fail.

Because sports appeals to a large number of people, the latest sports headlines become a good starting point for small talk conversations. Even if you ask, "What did you think about the game last night?" and the response is, "I don't know, I didn't watch." You've still got a potential line of questioning that makes more sense than asking what kind of vegetable they'd like to be. In that specific example, you could follow up with, "What did you have going on last night?"

That conversation could go in any number of ways, but in each case, you'll be learning more about the person you're talking to and gaining intel on possible conversation topics in the future. It takes time to build relationships. Using a topic with staying power (like sports) gives you opportunities to stay on the radar.

If you already talk sports at work, keep it up! If it's not something you naturally talk about, start building your sports knowledge base: read local sports headlines to become familiar with teams, names and topics that are relevant to your city (and likely to be on the radar of your sports-loving colleagues).

Sports Watch and Talk

Listen to postgame interviews with a more critical ear. Pay attention to the questions being asked and the way a player or coach responds. First, determine if the question generated an answer that provided information. Secondly, decide how you might answer the same question. Third, if your reaction to a question like, "How does it feel to win a championship?" is, "What kind of question is that? How do you think it feels!" come up with a better way to ask a question that gets less of a "No shit, Sherlock" response.

Task

Use postgame interviews as a reminder to apply the same critical ear to the conversations you have at work. Think about a conversation you plan to have in the next couple days. Say it out loud, start with the same point of reference, avoid no-duh questions and make sure you can not only say the words, but that they are the right ones to say.

Chapter in a Tweet...or Two

"An Influential Conversationalist considers how the other person is receiving the information and the general context of the situation."

"When you've invested time in getting to know people, they'll invest good faith back in you, according to @JenTalksSports"

CHAPTER 4

Cheering Versus Rooting

How important are good conversation skills? It can be the difference in getting a job or not in the NFL.

Every year when the NFL Combine rolls around, the hype usually follows the fastest 40-yard dash time or new record set on the bench press. Hours of television time gets devoted to showing college players performing specific drills for their potential employers. But that's not where draft day decisions are made.

"We don't care so much about the numbers, it's the interview process," one NFL scout explained. After researching a player for several months, scouts know what they're getting from the *athlete,* but they want to know what they're getting from the *person.* There are rules prohibiting scouts from talking to players while in college. The combine is the first time they can actually hear from the player himself.

It's a given that if a player is at the combine he's got physical talent. That's a no-brainer. But what else does he bring to the table? That's what scouts want to know.

"I know I can write you a million dollar check on the field. Can I trust you to write you a million dollar check off the field? Football character and personal character are separate grades, but both very important. We're worried about the personal grade at the combine, not the football one."

Just like it's a no-brainer that a football player has talent if they're attending the NFL Combine, it's a no-brainer that you're in your job, or being considered for a job, because of your talent. Like the NFL's "football grade," your degrees, resume, previous work history and professional accomplishments are like your "work grade." What about your personal grade? NFL players have them—so do you. You might not think of it that way, but it's definitely a consideration for your employer and your colleagues. Your off-the-chart talent or smarts are only part of what gets you, or keeps you in, a job. Your personal impact is what develops your fanbase at work.

Putting the Fan in "Fanatic"

If you want people—like your colleagues—to actively support you, cheer for you and become fans not just of your work, but of you—there's more to be done than your job.

There's a difference between someone being a fan of *you* versus being a fan of *your work*. Just like there's a difference between cheering for an athlete versus actively rooting for them. A sports fan cheers for the guy who leads the league in touchdown receptions because it's silly not to when that guy is on "your team." That same fan could have more of a rooting interest in the less productive, second-string receiver who was an undrafted free agent, coming back from a broken leg. The difference? The story. The connection points. The personal interest. It leads to more than a reason to cheer: it's a reason to root.

As a member of the Seattle Mariners broadcast team it's actually part of my job to cultivate that rooting interest by fans. How do you do that? You either get the player away from the baseball field or get them talking about something other than baseball.

It's one thing for a fan to see a baseball player in highlights or during the game broadcast. It's another to feel like you know him on a deeper level. Fans connect on a personal and emotional level. That only happens when they can get the story behind a player's success (or "productivity" as you might call it in a business setting). Give fans a little insight on a player's personality or personal journey—and watch out world! That's when you experience the full emotion and support that puts the "fan" in "fanatics."

Fans need to actually hear from, and relate to, the player. That's when they cross over from expressing a casual interest to passionate rooting.

The same is true for you.

Your colleagues need a way to relate to you and really hear from you. If the only thing you ever talk about is work, you create a group of casual observers around you. When you open up and relate on topics outside of work you're developing "fans" who will support you, cheer for you and could one day even advocate for you.

Conversations help identify connection points with your colleagues. You have to be willing to have a discussion, engage in a little small talk and be prepared with some substance in your answers.

Let's refer back to the interviews taking place at the NFL Combine. When I pressed an NFL scout on what a team is looking for in a player's response, he offered a couple examples of what not to do:

"It's a given that everyone at the combine is trying to get better," he told me. "So when you ask a player, 'What are you doing to get better?' and they say, 'Work hard every day.' Nah. That's what your agent told you to say. What are *you* doing to get better?"

The Lesson: A vague answer is almost worse than none at all. There are no details. No substance. No emotion. No connection point.

Here's what the scout really wanted to know: "Can you be a real dude at the combine and not some stiff in a suit? Can I relate to you?"

Remember, the scouts already have all the physical information and stats (basically the on-field resume) for each player. They're looking for answers that provide additional perspective about what the athlete could bring to the table. And if you don't think that matters, consider the example he gave when I asked about an answer that stood out during a round of interviews:

"We asked a player the simple question, 'why should we draft you?' He was a highly acclaimed player. We asked why we should draft him and his answer was, 'because I'm a nice guy.'"

That response didn't go over well.

"'I'm a nice guy' as the answer? That's not going to work." He said, shaking his head at the memory.

Remember, the player was in a high-leverage job interview with a team who was potentially willing to pay him a lot of money to work for them and he offered a generic four-word answer that didn't do anything to convince the team to draft him. The scout was frustrated by the response because he expected (and wanted) to hear about the value the player brought to the team, both in skillset and personality. Explaining how he's approached his off-season like a professional and describing his training routine would have been one way to do that.

It doesn't seem like the answer to that question should be the deal breaker, but consider a friend of mine who landed a job with her response to a similar one. She was interviewing for a job when she was 20-years old. She thought the meeting would be with the hiring manager and didn't anticipate being walked to a table with about a dozen high-level staff (including the owner of the company) who promptly started the job interview with the question, "Why you?" Everyone turned and stared. Her witty and off-the-cuff response of "Cutting right to the chase—I like that! I know this company is number one in the area, and I want to be part of your team—I will do everything it takes to earn my place on it every single day." gave her future employer the insight they needed on her personality.

When a team (or employer) is asking what value they will get from you if they draft (or hire) you, there needs to be a more concrete response that demonstrates why you are a good fit.

You need colleagues to be fans of you as a person (as much as they are of your work) because productivity only gets you so far. Just like an NFL scout, your coworkers want to know if they can relate to you, because that's required to build rapport and establish trust. Yeah, they know you can do the work, but what are you like to work *with*?

This does not mean you have to open up and share every detail of your personal life. (Please, don't do that. It doesn't make you relatable. It makes you an over-sharer and likely someone offering too much information.)

What you need is an easy entry point into a conversation, allowing you to reveal limited personal information in a comfortable setting. You need sports conversations.

Why?

Well, I've written an entire book on the subject of using sports conversations in business. *Talk Sporty to Me: Thinking Outside the Box Scores* covers it in greater detail, but here's the abbreviated version:

Sports works because it's a topic that interests millions of people in the United States based on yearly Gallup Poll surveys. Given those numbers, your workplace is likely filled with a high percentage of sports fans.

In addition, sports fans like talking about sports. They also enjoy conversations with other people who either talk sports or allow them to talk sports. This gives you an easy starting point.

Sports is a safe subject that keeps you away from hot-button topics like money, religion, politics, sex, or a boring topic like the weather. (Please stay away from sports stories that include hot-button issues. There are plenty of other options in the wide world of sports.)

Lastly, a sports conversation makes it easier to control the amount of information you reveal about yourself and the way you present that information.

For example, you can't walk up to a coworker, ask if they want to know more about you and launch into your life story starting with the swim lessons you took when you were three years old, the birthday cake fiasco when you were five or the heartbreak of not getting accepted to your first choice college when you were 17.

Let's be real. That's not what your colleagues want to hear and it's not helpful in building your fanbase at work.

Here's what you could do instead. Ask if anyone saw the basketball game the previous night and then mention you keep tabs on the Dallas Mavericks because you grew up in Texas and went to school in Dallas. That's not only a reasonable explanation as to why you follow a certain team, but it gives coworkers a little more insight on who you are, where you came from and provides opportunities for them to ask you follow up questions about your childhood or college days. (Even then, I'd advise you to still skip the part about swim lessons and the birthday cake fiasco. If you feel the need to mention the college acceptance heartbreak, don't dwell on it.)

If you're thinking, "Why don't I just skip the sports talk stuff and start asking coworkers where they're from? Eventually they'll ask me the same question and I'll have a chance to talk to them that way."

You could do that and it might work. Here are some other things that might happen: it might lead to a much-longer-than-necessary conversation about their child-hood birthday cake fiasco. It might turn into a dead-end conversation leaving you with little to come back to in a later interaction. And they might not have the aware-ness to ask you the question in return.

Introducing sports as a small talk topic provides more follow up opportunities, reduces the chance of dead-end conversations and puts you in the driver's seat.

Control what you can control.

Starting a conversation is certainly something with-in your control.*

As is having a plan once you're actually in the

---

* If you need specific help on starting a sports conversation, sign up at **TalkSportytoMe.com** to receive a weekly list of sports conversation starters right to your inbox.

conversation. Think about what you want to say ahead of time. What pieces of personal information would give your colleagues insights into who you are? Consider hometown, favorite teams, college alma mater, hobbies, family, or the first job you ever had. Each of those things reveals something different about what makes you, "you" and gives them an opportunity to connect, build rapport and ultimately root you on.

Influential Conversationalist Strategy

Make yourself relatable. Talk to your colleagues about something other than work. To that end, make a plan ahead of time on how to use sports to bring up personal talking points like your hometown, favorite type of food, hobbies, kids or pets. Have an idea of what you're going to say, but don't give rehearsed answers.

Remember, there needs to be substance or it's no different than the football player who failed to impress NFL scouts with a canned answer given to him by his agent.

Sports Watch and Talk

Athletes are known for more than the role they play in sports. Their personalities play a role in why and how they become fan favorites. Sometimes a fan is drawn to their community involvement, other times it's because of a shared experience like learning you both took piano lessons at a young age.

When an athlete piques your interest, make a mental note of why you find that player intriguing or attention worthy. What did he or she do, outside of the game, that caught your attention? If it's something you have in common, use it to start a conversation with a colleague that makes both you and the athlete relatable.

> "I didn't realize Randy Johnson was into photography until the broadcasters made mention of it during the game last night. I'm taking a photography workshop next month, but it looks like I've got a long way to go to match Randy."

A conversation like that indicates you've got an interest in both photography and sports. You've provided multiple follow up opportunities and way for your colleague to talk to you about something other than work.

Chapter in a Tweet...or Two

"Your personal impact is what develops your fanbase at work via @JenTalksSports"

"According to @JenTalksSports your colleagues want to know the same thing an NFL scout does: "Can I relate to you?""

CHAPTER 5

Less Talk, More Action

Seems out of place for me to advocate a strategy involving talking less in a book about being an Influential Conversationalist...but hear me out. We get really good at talking about what we want to do. The dream job we want to have. The company we want to work for. The salary we want to be paid. There's merit in all of those conversations, but each one is more productive if you invest time into the process.

The previous chapter highlighted the importance of having colleagues who not only liked your work, but liked you. You need a way for people to relate to you and you need to give them time to become fans of yours. It takes more than one game to develop a passionate sports fan. Clearly, it's going to take a lot more for a colleague or manager to develop a rooting interest in your success (See Chapter 4).

Your ability to implement new conversation techniques gets you noticed from the get go, but Influential Conversationalists have staying power. So do the best leaders.

*You need to show up and do great work all
the time for others to see you as a leader.
Leaders show up consistently, even before
they're in a leadership position.*

Showing up consistently includes everything from your demeanor (are you generally pleasant to be around?) to your willingness to have regular conversations (do you only talk to people when you need something or are you putting in the daily work needed to develop relationships?) and physically show up (are you where you need to be seen?).

I've personally seen the importance of showing up in my career, and have a Super Bowl ring to show for it.

The Story Behind the Super Bowl Ring

I was standing on the Seahawks sideline prior to Super Bowl 48, running through my notes and talking to myself in preparation for a pregame report. My phone buzzed. It was a message from my college roommate that read, "Congratulations roomie! You've come a long way from using me as your first interview in school. You don't have to play in the game for it to be a big accomplishment. Have fun!"

She was right. It was a big accomplishment that got even bigger a few months later when I received my own Super Bowl ring celebrating the Seattle Seahawks' win against the Denver Broncos. I don't break out the bling very often, but when I do people always ask how I ended up with one in the first place. The short answer is, I am a part of the Seahawks radio broadcast team, and owner Paul Allen was gracious in including us among those who received rings.

The longer, more detailed answer is: I showed up. Every chance I got. I showed up to practices, press conferences, games and even used a week of vacation on two separate occasions to go to training camp and show up for 8-10 hours a day and work. (Before you go get any crazy ideas about stalking someone you want to work for, let me back up and explain: at the time I was working for a local TV affiliate in Seattle as a sports producer. As such, I had press credentials and was allowed to attend all practices, press conferences, games and training camps.) My hours at the TV station were 3:00-11:30pm. The hours before work were the ones I trucked myself to the Seahawks facility to watch practice and listen to then-coach Mike Holmgren tell stories during his weekly press conferences.

Here's what I was clear in communicating—I wanted the chance to audition for the sideline reporter job *if it ever came open.* Someone else already had the job and she was great at it. I thought given my background as a high school football official and my experience in broadcasting I could be a good fit for the job if the opportunity arose. I expressed my interest to the folks who would make that determination and then I showed up everywhere they looked.

I did that for six years before I had the opportunity to audition and interview for the job. At that point, there were probably a few people who already thought I was a part of the organization because I was around All. The. Time.

As a result, acing an interview and audition was no big deal. I had spent six years building relationships with everyone I'd be working with, including the players and coaches. I wasn't worried about the questions they would ask in an interview. I didn't have to be nervous about an audition. I knew how to handle it and they knew me because I consistently showed up for years.

Every time I look at that ring with my name on it, I'm reminded my approach paid off. It took a while and there certainly were times I felt like I was running myself ragged for nothing. It wasn't for nothing. I was developing relationships and being evaluated every step of the way.

Here's my advice: Take your Influential Conversation skills and put yourself in a position to talk to key influencers and decision makers over and over (and over) again.

Be seen to the point that people don't remember the space without you.

Technology makes it possible to show up in all kinds of ways in business. You can show up in an email, video conference, conference call, phone call, or instant message...but none can match the value of showing up in person.

Let me put this another way: sit at your desk. If you have a desk to work at, stop trying to find a way to work remotely.

I know this is an unpopular thing to say. I understand some companies are structured so everyone works remotely. What I want you to understand is this: there is no substitute for real human interaction. Video conferencing is a fantastic tool, allowing people to connect visually. You're still not getting the same experience.

Please don't think I'm anti-email or text message. I take part in countless conference calls and sometimes video conferencing is the best way to connect across time zones. There's value in all those forms of communication. Just remember, the more you show up in person the more people see you as the total package.

Here's why you should physically show up as often as you can:

Communication Improves. This includes everything from small talk, to nonverbal communication and the actual work conversations you have over the course of the day. The more time you spend around someone, the easier it is to strike up a conversation and know how to deliver information to them.

"You gotta know who you're working with and that comes over time and over years." Said Seahawks linebacker K.J. Wright. "[You learn] how well they can process things before the play, if they like a lot of information or just a little. It's just part of growing with one another."

Part of that happens through repetition on the field. But being in the same space, regardless of the activity, has a lot to do with developing that knowledge.

"The more you spend time with guys, the more you understand them. That's why it's important to have defensive dinners where all the guys go out, have linebacker night—it all pays off because we know each other."

Response to Adversity. At some point, you're going to fail. It doesn't matter how talented you are, you're going to deal with adversity, and key influencers want to see your response. It's no different than an NFL team wanting to know how a player is going to react to having a bad game or a bad season. It's going to happen, they want to know he can handle it. Here's how an NFL scout related it back to business.

"How do you respond when you thought you were getting that job but someone else got it? Are you going to be pissed off and motivated to show them you should have gotten the job, or are you going to sit there and pout for the next six months because that should have been your job and now you're not going to work?"

It's not fun to think about failure or disappointment, but you want the key influencers you work with to see you've got the grit to respond to adversity—and the communication skills to match.

React and Adjust. Like dealing with adversity, you need to demonstrate your ability to react and adjust. It's like a pitcher and catcher who go into the game with a specific game plan and find themselves needing to adjust midway through an inning.

"You have to be able to process a lot of information—and then not get bogged down by it—and make quick decisions." Arizona Diamondbacks catcher Chris Iannetta explained, "You have to make adjustments when the visual reads you get differ from what you expect. You have to be able to make adjustments on the fly, and that's what makes you a good game caller."

This is also a valuable skillset to have in business. When you're seen making quick adjustments, communicating effectively and not being overwhelmed by changing information or circumstances, it reinforces your status as an Influential Conversationalist.

Mentors Become Obvious. Please stop looking for mentors. They're sitting right next to you at work, at lunch and at networking functions. They're everywhere you are. You'll discover that when you show up and start talking to the people around you.

Let me be clear—I believe in mentorship. I don't believe in asking for a mentor.

Here's what I've noticed about the recent trend: getting a mentor is being treated as something that can be checked off a to-do list. Once a mentor is identified, that person is treated as someone responsible for fast-tracking a mentee's career. That's not how it works.

I have mentors. I'm happy to be a mentor, but it requires work. The same work that it takes to build a relationship. That's how I got my mentors. I asked questions, I bought them coffee. I stayed late. I worked extra. I was a pest. I'm sure they wanted me to go away but I continued to show up. I worked my butt off. I put myself in a position to get the best opportunities in my career. I couldn't have done it without my mentors and champions, but they wouldn't have done it without my persistence and committed insistence toward building the relationship.

I had to be available. I had to show up.

No Timetable

I can't tell you how long it's going to take before you show up enough to get your dream job. In the case of my Super Bowl ring story it took six years. In the case of my television career it took 10 years. The only thing I know for sure is there is no shortcut and there's no substitute for showing up.

As frustrating as it might seem, time and experience work in your favor. It allows you to hone your skillset and allows people around you to evaluate your skills. NFL players know that. Based on 2017 statistical data, the average career of an NFL player is 3.3 years. If there's anyone who would want to find a shortcut to success it would be them...except that's not how these guys approached it. Do you know what they said when they wanted to step into larger roles, be seen as leaders and be given more responsibility? Show up and be consistent.

Kam Chancellor, Seahawks Safety

"If it's something that you love to do show your passion. The only way someone can tell you love what you do is by your passion. So, you gotta put all your passion into what you do, give it all you got. You gotta show it and people feed off it."

Richard Sherman, Seahawks Cornerback

"In sports, you put extra time in—in the gym, on the field—and it shows. It always shows. Hard work is never quiet. You can see a guy work all summer and he goes out there and it's not like you're going to say, 'Oh he didn't do anything this summer.' It shows. It's shows if you worked hard, it shows if you're dedicated to your craft— if you put in the work."

Bobby Wagner, Seahawks Linebacker

"Sometimes you do have to wait your turn. Sometimes you have older guys with more experience—guys who have been in it longer and all these different things, and it's not quite your turn yet. But the best thing I think you can do is continue to work on yourself and continue to better yourself, and that's what I did. I just continued to lead by example. You don't have to say much. If you go out and do the things you're supposed to do it can't be ignored. That consistency can't be ignored. Your time will come when it's supposed to come."

K.J. Wright, Seahawks Linebacker

"I showed up. Whatever task is at hand you get the job done and the coaches start to trust you. And your teammates start to trust you. And with that comes more responsibilities. Just start at the beginning doing that, and as you grow and get older they'll ask you to do different stuff to see if you can handle that and do your job."

Here's the gist of what all these guys are telling you: "Saying something isn't as effective as *doing* something."

Here's what the Influential Conversationalists knows: You can't say something one time and expect doors to open. You've got to combine words with actions that leave no doubt in the minds of the people you're working with.

Influential Conversationalist Strategy

Leaders are asked to excel at tasks big and small, and show up consistently. That means being consistent in your demeanor and physically showing up. Every day.

You can demonstrate consistency in lots of different ways. It starts by just showing up and having a conversation every day. You want people to see you in the same place giving the same effort.

Practice Being Friendly and Approachable. Say "Hi" when you come into work and walk to your desk. Make it part of your routine and it will be easier to stay consistent when you're in a bad mood or not feeling particularly chipper about being at work.

Practice Smiling. You might not realize your "deep in thought" look comes across as you frowning at colleagues. Make a concerted effort to smile throughout the day. Try to catch yourself in the mirror (or in the reflection on your computer screen). What's the natural look on your face? If it's anything other than pleasant and approachable, set a smile reminder a couple times a day on your phone to get used to practicing that look. You want to make it easy for people to talk to you and see you as a leader. It's hard to do that if it looks like you're consistently in a bad mood. Who wants to work with (or for) a grump?

Sports Watch and Talk

It's not hard to identify sports examples that highlight consistency, staying-power and long-term success. Teams with those qualities are considered dynasties. Players with those characteristics are said to be future Hall of Famers.

Listen to how both are described during broadcasts. Or lean on your own knowledge of watching a coach win games for over a decade. Or a player adapting his/her style to dominate for 12 years in a league where the average career lasts less than five.

If you're looking for a way to highlight the importance of consistency amongst the people you work with, try starting with a sports example, like:

"Mike Krzyzewski has been the head coach at Duke for over 30 years, but he still wouldn't have been able to win over 1,000 games without consistency in the guys he recruited and in his overall approach. I think we need to develop a more consistent approach in prospecting clients to start finding more success."

Chapter in a Tweet...or Two

"Take your Influential Conversation skills and put yourself in position to talk to key influencers and decision makers over and over again."

"Show up over a period of time. Do great work all the time. Leaders show up consistently, even before they're in a leadership position."

CHAPTER 6

Be Interesting

If you want people to talk to you (or listen to you) it helps if you're interesting. Here's one way to become the most interesting person in the room—experience.

I often get asked about the most interesting players or people I've interviewed. In general, I'm intrigued and interested by people who have some life experience. Sometimes it's the high-profile athlete, other times it's the person behind the scenes you've never heard of. In any case, life experience (and the perspective that comes as a result of it) are what makes someone interesting to talk to.

No one seeks out a boring person to have a conversation with every day. When you're interesting people want to talk to you. More than that, when you've got perspective and insight (and consistently share it well), people will specifically seek you out for conversations. In both cases, you increase your visibility and influence.

Gaining experience requires time, failure, and honest conversations. Up to this point, we've talked about how an Influential Conversationalist talks to others. Now, it's time to look at the conversations you need to have with yourself.

Career Development

Want to know the reason it's called career "development?" Because you are not a finished product. There's always something to learn, a new skill to obtain, a talent to develop and a way to get better. Where you start isn't where you're going to finish.

Even if you've just landed your dream job, like college football players being drafted by an NFL team, there's still work to do. Just take a look at the draft evaluations from a few NFL players:

- On Seahawks safety Kam Chancellor

  "Chancellor can play over aggressive at times, take poor angles and is susceptible to play fakes."

- On Seahawks cornerback Richard Sherman:

  "Tall, high-cut prospect who displays some hip-stiffness. Not explosive when transitioning or when changing direction."

- On Seahawks linebacker Bobby Wagner:

    "Wagner is undersized to play middle linebacker in the NFL."

- On Seahawks linebacker K.J. Wright:

    "Wright's recognition skills and overall awareness need improvement. Has trouble with quicker tight ends and backs in man coverage."

If you didn't know any better, you might think those players were set up to fail. Except every single one them became a Super Bowl Champion, developed into a Pro Bowl player and became one of the most feared players on one of the best defenses in the NFL.

Either the "experts" didn't know what they were talking about *or* the experts were right for a moment in time and the players improved, developed their skills and advanced past where they started. Perhaps it's a little of both. And perhaps you can relate to these Pro Bowlers.

Every one of those guys had a desire to succeed in the NFL. Each of them had the talent to get drafted, which gave them a foot in the door with an NFL team. All of them took their initial opportunities, grew into larger rolls and developed into incredible players.

It's called career development for a reason. And, I'm sorry to tell you there's no set time on how long development takes. It is different for every person and situation. Yes, that can be frustrating, but it's also something you can influence.

Talk Yourself Into It

"You gotta enjoy the journey." Seahawks linebacker K.J. Wright said emphatically when I asked why he wouldn't want to skip the years between being an NFL rookie to being a Pro Bowl veteran.

"Everything is a journey and the end will come, but when you're going through what you're going through you just gotta do it. You just gotta enjoy it. You can't just skip to greatness—you've got to take those baby steps and [success] will come on its own."

"It's the same mindset in business," Doug Baldwin, Seahawks wide receiver says. "If you enjoy the journey, and take pride in the journey, and enjoy the roller coaster effect of it, the ups and downs—be thankful for the journey. Be grateful for it, because it's teaching you valuable lessons whether you win or you lose. And it will bring you to a greater success or goal."

Career development isn't a haphazard thing. You might not be able to control the final outcome, but you can definitely control the steps you take and the conversations you have with yourself along the way. Here's the other thing you need to realize about career development: as much as you want others to notice your skills, as much as you want to put yourself in a position to talk about your successes—some of the most critical conversations you'll have are with yourself.

An Influential Conversationalist needs to be able to have tough conversations with him or herself.

You might be fortunate to work for a manager who recognizes your talent and articulates the exact steps needed to work your way into a dream job. You still need to figure out a few things first and decide what you're willing to do. Start with this list:

Be Specific About the End Result. Most people put more thought into planning their weekly grocery list than their career plan. Think about it. You should have some clarity and specificity around what you're trying to accomplish in your career. (It's pretty important after all.)

It would be unusual to hear an NFL player say his goal is to play one snap in an NFL game. It's just as ridiculous to think your goal is to get any ol' job that comes your way. Without knowing what you really want, or the things on your list, you won't be able to find the best-fit opportunities.

While you're thinking about that end-result goal, make sure you know what it entails as far as responsibilities, qualifications and demands on your time. For example, do you want to keep a strict 9-to-5, Monday through Friday schedule, and "unplug" on the weekends? If so, you're probably not a candidate for a high level leadership position that requires you to be accessible seven days a week, solve problems when they come up (which could be at an inconvenient time) and attend weekly 8am leadership meetings.

Be Honest With Your Self-Evaluation. Despite what your parents or grade school teachers told you, it's very unlikely you can be anything you want to be. There are limitations to what you can do. This isn't a bad thing, it's a reality thing. Seahawks wide receiver Doug Baldwin grappled with this very issue early in his career and was forced to be super honest about his abilities.

"I used to watch film of Randy Moss and Terrell Owens before I got into the NFL, and I had to look at myself in mirror and say, 'Doug you're not 6'3", 6'4" you don't run a 4.3-40. That's not you.' I had to direct my passion and my goals. I started looking at guys who were similar to me, like Steve Smith. Basically, it came down to me looking in the mirror and saying what am I capable of?"

To add a little more context to this, Baldwin is 5'10' and a slot receiver. Here's the difference, slot receivers use quickness and shiftiness to get open in the middle of the field. Outside receivers like Moss and Owens use their size and speed to get down the field and get open. Both are necessary, important roles to be filled on the team—by the right person.

Prior to his self-evaluation he was studying guys who had a different body type and different skill set. Trying to emulate Moss and Owens wouldn't have worked for Baldwin because he's not the same type of receiver. No matter how hard he tried, he was never going to have their skillset, so he embraced his. You need to do the same. Determine your proficiencies and talents. Be honest with yourself or you'll end up frustrated in the end.

Let's think about this in another way. I frequently hear from people who want to "do what I do" and become a sports broadcaster. Some of those people have shared that they're afraid of being on camera and are intimidated to talk to people. Both of which are required for doing my job. They can still pursue the path of working in sports broadcasting, but their best fit is probably in a behind-the-scenes job.

Essentially, you are probably never going to be a doctor if you were squeamish in 7th grade science class, but that doesn't mean you can't work in medicine or help people...which leads us to the next point:

Be Open to Adjacent Opportunities. Chances are, you're not going to land your dream job on the first try. You might not be qualified for it initially or even know what the exact title is. That doesn't mean you sit around and wait for something to happen. Start moving in a direction that gets you closer to your goal even if it's not exactly what you wanted to do.

Seahawks safety Kam Chancellor wanted to be a running back as a young player, then he wanted to be a quarterback. It wasn't until he got to college that his coach moved him to safety: the position he was drafted to play in the NFL. And one he excels at so much for the Seahawks he helped redefine it for the entire league.

Chancellor wouldn't have had the opportunity to find his dream job without his time spent as a running back and quarterback. Being on the football field, being around the game, opened the right doors.

Mariners infielder Shawn O'Malley broke into the big leagues as a utility player, but that's not what he dreamed of being. (If you aren't familiar with the term, the utility player is sort of a jack of all trades.)

"I always wanted to be a shortstop. I remember watching Alex Rodriguez and I remember thinking, 'Yeah, I could do that.'" O'Malley said. "That's what I wanted to be. But the older I got, the more experienced I got, I realized that's not the way I was going to break into the big leagues. So, I would go out of my way to take ground balls and take fly balls with conviction."

The opportunity wasn't there for Shawn to get into the big leagues in the way he dreamt of as a child. That didn't mean he quit baseball, it meant he looked for another way to get on the field. Becoming a utility player, a guy who can play multiple positions but is not generally used as an everyday starter, was an adjacent opportunity that got him to his goal of becoming a big-league baseball player.

Cleaning ballpark bathrooms and scooping up beer-soaked peanut shells by hand were a few of my adjacent opportunities. Trust me, I was not in love with every step of my career journey. I was, however, thrilled to spend an entire summer while in college working for a minor league baseball team. Take the good with the bad, and recognize without a few challenges or crummy job responsibilities people don't know what you're made of. Heck, you don't know what you're made of.

Where are your adjacent opportunities? What job gets you in the vicinity of the right industry and decision makers?

Be in a Position to Fail. You aren't going to learn unless you not only have the ability to fail, but do so on a regular basis. It's not an easy conversation to have with yourself, because we don't often look at the successful side of failing. Seahawks All Pro cornerback Richard Sherman does: "Going through adversity you learn a lot about yourself—figure out how to react and move in situations. [You learn] how you affect others and how you can affect other situations."

It sounds crazy to say, but you want to be in position to fail in little ways on a regular basis. Working in live television gives me plenty of opportunities to "fail" and follow it up with a success. I might make a mistake early in a pregame show by flubbing a line or forgetting a piece of information I needed to say. But less than five minutes later I could have the chance to come back with a solid report. I've got a safe space to make a mistake—one that isn't crucial, detrimental to the company or harmful to anyone—and get better as a result.

Sherman gets that experience as an NFL player. Make a mistake on one play and there's an opportunity to come back and do better on the very next one. It's the same opportunity he had in Pee Wee football, and something an athlete at any level can appreciate.

"Playing sports hardens you mentally in some ways and helps you deal with [adversity], because you deal with the lows," Sherman explained. "If your team lost the game, or they've lost every game, you deal with how to cope with that in your everyday life. Then you deal with the other side: in winning a whole bunch of games, and making a game winning shot, and being successful. You understand that's not final. That's not definitive and you should treat them the same."

"I think sports is a good parallel to life," he continued, "and the unexpected things, and the adversity that can come during your lifetime and how you react to that. Every time you reach adversity you can choose to react a certain way, and how you react defines your path."

I couldn't have said it any better than Sherman. You might not want to face adversity or acknowledge you're going to be anything but brilliant at work. Trust me (and Sherman). You need to fail. You need to have the opportunity to make mistakes, develop a way to bounce back and become better as a result.

Let me be clear as we bring this back to a corporate

or business setting: you should not be looking for ways to cause harm to the company or cause other people to fail. This is about you and honing your skills for a potential climb up the ladder. How can you stretch outside your comfort zone? Force yourself into low leverage, safe situations where you don't always have the answers.

In your work life, let's go back to the water cooler or coffee run examples. You will not have stellar encounters every single time, especially right off the bat. Try some out (hopefully you have been taking notes and attempting the tasks I have provided at the end of each chapter so far) and make little adjustments to get better. If you flub a water cooler conversation, who cares?

The thing you said that seemed like a huge deal to you...probably wasn't that big of a deal to the other person. Can you remember a time someone came over to apologize for something stupid they said to you three days ago, and you couldn't remember the conversation? It had been eating them up inside, but it didn't even make a blip on your radar. Yes, some things can be a big deal, but for the most part you can move on and not dwell.

Be Able to Tell Yourself What to Do. Are you going through the motions or do you know exactly what you need to do, and why? Critical thinking and being able to coach yourself are part of developing leadership skills.

NFL coaches aren't part of the huddle before plays, but K.J. Wright's internal running commentary keeps him on track and focused. "I preach to myself 'good depth, so don't get close to the line,'" Wright says. "When I'm in coverage, I tell myself 'stay square, stay square.' If there's a certain formation a team always runs a certain play out of, I tell myself it's coming. Those are the main things I tell myself: 'good depth, stay square and anticipate the history of ball play.' "

If you want to be able to coach someone else up, you need to be able to do it for yourself first.

The conversations you have with yourself can make all the difference in the caliber and size of your next career opportunity. While you are doing that, make sure to keep an eye out for small things that can make a big difference.

Consider the employee who met with the CEO of the company he worked for and expressed a desire to become a CEO one day.

> "The first thing I'd do is shine your shoes," the CEO responded.

> "What?" the employee asked as he looked down at his scuffed shoes.

> "If you want to be a CEO you need to look the part," replied the CEO.

The meeting ended, the employee left. He never shined his shoes. He apparently thought it wasn't a task big enough to make a difference…except the CEO noticed every time they passed in the hall or sat in a meeting.

I wonder if the employee realized he was sending a message with those scuffed shoes, one that said "I'm not interested in following advice, and it's not important to me to do the little things I'm asked to do." I also wonder if the employee realizes the CEO would have been willing to give him a shot at proving he was ready for more responsibility had he just shined his shoes. Instead, every time he saw those scuffed shoes, the CEO just shrugged and thought, "I guess you didn't really want to be a CEO."

The CEO in that story is my father, and he used that story in a conversation with me to illustrate ways you can show up and lead regardless of where you are in an organization.

If you're looking for your big moment to shine, you're probably missing the plethora of small opportunities right in front of you.

The little tasks are your test.
The big tasks are your reward.

As I've told interns for years, if I can't trust you to do little things right, why would I ever give you responsibility for something more?

If you want the chance to do more, you better be willing to do what you've been asked or told in the first place. Even if it's not important to you. If someone asked you to do something, there is a reason. Perhaps it's important someone else sees you're detailed oriented, or that you're capable of following instructions. Guess what? Leaders are asked to do both.

Develop your skills. Enjoy the journey of getting to where you're going. You'll be there soon enough.

Oh, and don't forget to shine your shoes.

Influential Conversationalist Strategy

There is no substitute for experience in your career development or in your conversation habits. Looking for the shortcut stunts your development. Not only because you're wasting time looking for a shortcut in the first place, but because you're going to end up making mistakes in highly visible positions.

Find a scenario that allows you to practice having conversations throughout the day, including with people you don't know. For example, make it a point to say "Hello" to someone in an elevator, or make small talk while standing in line for coffee. Make sure those conversations occasionally involve people you don't know. As an Influential Conversationalist, you need to be able to handle conversations with lots of different people. You're not always going to have the luxury of researching the person you're talking to, developing a line of questioning ahead of time or rehearsing what you're going to say. Practice not being caught off guard by working on your conversation skills right now. If the conversation doesn't go smoothly, no problem. You were just waiting in line for coffee and now you're going your separate ways. It's a way to practice before you find yourself in a make or break situation requiring you to entertain new clients at the request of your CEO.

Sports Watch and Talk

"Players to watch" type segments are popular features throughout the world of sports. Those segments or articles involve topics like identifying up-and-coming talent and spotlighting players who are stepping into larger roles.

In many cases, the story will contain a mention of where the player has come from (meaning what talent level they started with) and then go on to explain how the player has grown into the ability to handle more responsibility. Somewhere in the story, a failure or shortcoming will serve as the launching point for a big improvement.

This is the hero archetype, and a story we love to watch unfold over and over again. Think of every hero in every story you have ever heard—they needed to overcome some shortcoming to save the day. You are the hero of your own story, so use this as a template for thinking about your career:

- What talents did you start with?

- Where have you seen the most growth?

- What was your biggest failure or shortcoming?

- How did you overcome it?

- In what area are you ready for more responsibility?

Utilize the answers in determining what opportunity you're looking for, or what "adjacent opportunity" could advance your career.

Chapter in a Tweet...or Two

"Your career development path starts with the conversations you have with yourself, according to @JenTalksSports"

"If you're looking for leadership opportunities, remember little tasks are your test. Big tasks are your reward."

CHAPTER 7

Does This Make
My Bias Look Big?

"Does this outfit make my butt look big?"

Admit it. You've either asked or been asked the question at least once in your life. I understand the importance of it (your butt looks just fine, by the way). The thing you should be worried about is how big your *bias* looks, because that has a direct impact on your career. It also shows up in the way you say things.

For example, the question, "As a woman, how much harder is it for you to succeed in your job?" is one I get asked a lot.

I hate that question. It really ticks me off.

Partly because it's not how I see the situation, and mostly because it signals you're looking for an excuse as to why something could be difficult. (You are trying to blame the refs again.) You assume it's harder for me to do my job than it is for a man in my same position.

It's not. That's your bias talking—which looks awfully

big when you ask me a question that starts with the phrase, "As a woman..."

I don't think about being a woman. I just get up and do my job. Just like my male counterparts and colleagues don't get up and think, "As a man, how am I going to approach my day?"

If you tell yourself you've got a tougher road ahead, you probably do. That doesn't make it true, it just means your bias is showing.

This is the point—if you're willing to assume my job is harder because I'm a woman, you're also more likely to believe something about your job or career opportunities that isn't true.

An Influential Conversationalist knows how to position conversations in a way that focuses on opportunities. Your bias against yourself can get in the way of your success more than anyone else's bias against you.

This is not a conversation about men versus women. The bias I have against myself has nothing to do with my gender.

My insecurities show up when I attempt to branch out from my core skillset. I know I'm good at talking, even to large groups or in live settings. However, I have a hard time convincing myself I can talk to a potential client and sell them one of my presentations and 50 copies of this book for the staff. Why? Because my degree, training and title have nothing to do with sales. Given how much I talk, and the expertise I have with the material, it's ridiculous to think I struggle with that...but I do.

The way I see it, I could look at my situation in one of two ways and say either, "As someone with a communications background instead of a business background, what did you expect, Jennifer?" (Yes, I did just refer to myself in third person and by my full name. It happens often when I get mad or frustrated at myself.) Or I could say, "Jennifer, you've got more experience talking in much higher leverage situations than a sales call. Stop being ridiculous and make the freakin' call."

It's not to say you can't ever have a qualifying statement as a way to make a comparison or gain context. For example, as someone who grew up in Texas, I don't think it's actually hot until the temperature reaches 90+ degrees. There is a difference, however, between prefacing a statement or question in a way that provides clarity to a situation, as opposed to making an excuse.

There are any number of contributing factors to the bias we show against ourselves and any of them can get in the way of being an effective leader. We're more likely to discredit ourselves, overlook opportunities and (in some cases) resist stepping into roles that were tailor made for us.

Seahawks safety Kam Chancellor did that. Anyone who knows the Pro Bowler and defensive captain, knows his leadership skills come naturally. You can see them simply from the way he carries himself in practice.

"There are people who are chosen to be leaders, like Kam," Seahawks teammate and fellow defensive captain Bobby Wagner said. "He can say 'No' all he wants, but if he was chosen to be a leader he's just fighting the inevitable."

Kam is a born leader. It was obvious to everyone from the time he played Pee Wee football. He speaks and his teammates follow. Except he didn't want to lead; didn't think he could because of how he viewed himself.

As a kid, Kam endured teasing at school and in the neighborhood over his hair, his skin color, his size. As a result, he resisted stepping into leadership roles for years.

"That was because of insecurity," Kam says with a smile as he thought back to his younger days. "That was insecurity, especially with myself and what people think when I talk."

It's hard to imagine anyone saying anything but, "Yes, sir!" to the 6'3", 225-pound man sitting next to me answering questions. His physical presence alone can command a room, but there's still a nervous chuckle in his voice as he described where the insecurity came from.

"That comes from my childhood: being joked as a kid about my cornrows or about my chapped lips, or about my big feet because I was skinny, or being joked about being dark-skinned," Kam explained. "All those different things made me not want to talk in front of people, because of being joked about those insecurities."

Today, Kam doesn't succumb to those doubts or

insecurities. In the years that followed, he grew into his hulking body, became a standout athlete and realized this: "Embrace everything that you have or that you're given. Sometimes you're young with big feet, big lips because you're going to be somebody humongous. Somebody fearless with a lot of tenacity who has a gift in whatever it is, and you're going to need what you were given to perform and be the best you can be."

In other words, the things Kam thought worked against him developed into some of his strongest assets. It took time, perspective and the reality of growing into his body to realize he needed to see the situation in a different light.

You control how you look at situations, position your skillsets, and talk about your experiences.

Here's something else to consider: you might think you're doing a good job of covering up your big bias, but you're probably not hiding it very well. Looking for excuses and reasons why you can't do something isn't attractive and doesn't gain the right kind of followers. Pay attention to the way you carry yourself.

"If you carry yourself in a way that attracts the right people, you're naturally going to be a leader." Bobby explained. "People are going to look up to you, be interested in the things you're doing and want to imitate and ask questions. In that sense, that is what leaders are. They've got a lot of people who look up to them and want their help. I feel that's really what leaders do. They help."

You can't do it if your bias gets in the way, or if you accept someone else's bias as truth. Every time I get asked one of those, "As a woman…" questions, I take a deep breath and point out it's not something I view as a challenge to overcome.

Instead I point out that because I am a woman, I have natural instincts and abilities that allow me to communicate effectively in locker rooms. I connect and build relationships easier than some of my male counterparts. And if I'm the only woman in a room full of men, who do you think everyone remembers?

Perhaps I am naïve in thinking my career path hasn't been harder than my male counterparts. Here's one thing I know for sure: no one I work with wants to hear excuses. Whining isn't allowed, and a big bias isn't going to get me anywhere.

Stop acting like an asterisk (you know, putting one of these * by your name because there's a footnote you want to explain about yourself) and looking for a way to qualify the difficulty of your success. Being successful is a challenge for everyone.

Get out of your own way and start taking advantage of the opportunities in front of you.

Influential Conversationalist Strategy

The conversations you have with yourself or about your abilities can influence the way you see your opportunities. We all deal with insecurities and self-doubt, but your perception isn't always reality. It's time to change the conversation.

List three examples of sentences you would start with, "As a...."

For example:

> "**As a** recent college graduate, I don't have enough experience to apply for the new job posting."

> "**As a** person who's worked in technology for 20 years, I don't have the same training as someone who works in sales."

For each statement you listed, replace the words, "As a..." with the words "Because I..."

> "**Because I** am a recent college graduate, I've got the drive to work long hours and implement new strategies they might not have considered."

> "**Because I** spent so much time working in technology, I know the ins

and outs of the products I'm selling
and am better equipped to answer any
questions from the potential buyers."

Those two words change not only the message you send, but the skills you're conveying about yourself. Be prepared with "Because I..." statements for the three biggest biases you demonstrate against yourself.

Sports Watch and Talk

No team goes into a game saying they don't have a chance. A team might know they're dealing with more injuries, or their opponent has a better record, or that odds-makers have given them little chance of winning. Instead of talking about the factors stacked against them, a coach or player will find areas that could favor them in the game. It might be a long-shot to believe them as a fan, but after nearly two decades in sports, some of the best examples I've seen of finding a silver lining come from underdog teams I've covered.

Those underdogs occasionally pull off upsets. The Seahawks did it against the Broncos in Super Bowl 48. Every year during March Madness a lower-ranked team knocks off an opponent that's better than them on paper. And the Chicago Cubs are no longer the "lovable losers" after winning the World Series in 2016 and ending a 108-year run without a title.

Pay attention to how the coach of an underdog team talks going into a game. The conversation isn't "As a team with more injuries than the other team." It sounds more like "Because we are dealing with more injuries, it's a chance for some of our other players to step up. I'm excited to see what they do with the opportunity."

Chapter in a Tweet...or Two

"If you tell yourself you've got a tougher road ahead, you probably do. That doesn't make it true—it just means your bias is showing"

"Don't look at the odds stacked against you. Focus on the opportunities right in front of you."

CHAPTER 8

Sexism Versus Poor Communication Skills

"Talks too much."

It was the phrase I saw written on every single report card. As in, "Jennifer is a good student, but she talks too much in class." Those comments prompted conversations at home about the importance of working at my desk without talking to the classmates around me. I would promise to do better and try hard to stay quiet. That resolve usually lasted until lunchtime the next day, when I was back to "talking too much."

Here's the thing about being the kid who talked too much. I don't think twice about speaking up at work— and it's very obvious to me when others do.

Being an Influential Conversationalist has a tangible impact on your career opportunities even though it doesn't show up on a resume.

Speak Up

The headline read, "Sexism in the workplace is worse than you thought." *

That's how a USA Today article described the findings of a LeanIn.org and McKinsey and Company report titled "Women in the Workplace."** The article highlighted key findings in the study, which concluded women were less likely to be promoted than men. A clear-cut case of sexism in the workplace if you look at these responses:

- Women who participated in the study said they were more likely to be ignored at meetings, with 67% of women saying they were "able to participate meaningfully" compared to 74% of men.

- The women also said they were less likely to get challenging assignments compared to their male counterparts.

- When it came to big decisions, women said they were less likely to be consulted for input. Only 56% of the women who participated said they were asked to share their thoughts in those situations, compared to 64% of men.

* https://www.usatoday.com/story/money/2016/09/27/lean-in-study-women-in-the-workplace/91157026/
** https://womenintheworkplace.com

The president of LeanIn.org commented on the study saying it, "clearly shows that women face an uneven playing field."

That's one way to look at it, but it's not the way I see it.

I read the article a couple times, but couldn't reach the same conclusion. The way I see it, the survey has very little to do with gender and everything to do with communication skills at work.

Here's why: none of those findings say the respondents aren't qualified to speak up at meetings, aren't ready to get challenging assignments or smart enough to be consulted on big decisions. That tells me the respondents have everything going for them—except their ability to communicate effectively at work.

It also tells me they're missing very obvious ways to control what they can control. Just take a look:

- Do you feel ignored at meetings? Speak up.

- Not getting challenging assignments? Talk to your manager, highlight your successes.

- Feeling left out of big decisions? Initiate conversations with your colleagues *before* your opinion counts.

Every one of those outcomes can be changed or influenced by becoming a better conversationalist and more effective communicator.

I know some of this is easier said than done, but I also know it's possible because as a sports broadcaster I talk for a living in the most male-dominated, testosterone-driven environment you can think of—professional locker rooms. Yes, I dealt with sexist comments when I was breaking into an industry that had relatively few females at the time. But, those types of interactions happened far less than the conversations I had with colleagues and the athletes I covered. What I've learned is this: my ability to communicate effectively in that environment evened the playing field for me (and still does).

Here's how I approach it:

Do You Feel Ignored at Meetings? Speak Up. Chaotic is the best word to describe the scene inside an NFL locker room after the game. Postgame interviews are rarely conducted in an orderly fashion and it's not unusual for me to be one of a large group of media members waiting to hear from a specific player. We all have questions, and if I want mine to be heard, I've got to be prepared, persistent and (occasionally) loud. If I stopped trying every time my question was "stepped on" (as in, someone else started talking while I was already talking) or talked over, I wouldn't have lasted very long in the business.

Speaking up is something Seahawks middle linebacker Bobby Wagner does in an even more extreme environment—the middle of the defensive huddle and over the din of 70,000 roaring fans on game day. Not only that, but he's got to get his teammates (some of whom are bigger, have more experience, and an even louder set of vocal chords) to listen. Wagner calls the defense. He is the person who verbalizes what his teammates need to be doing on the field during every play. He has to find a way to make his voice heard and capture the attention of everyone the huddle.

"You've got to approach with a level of confidence," Wagner explained. "How I went about it was knowing what I'm talking about. I have to be on everything, because you'll gain their respect, their trust."

Which is easier to do after a few years in the league, but Wagner had to do it as an unproven rookie in 2012 before earning any of the awards, accolades and franchise records destined to come his way. He made sure he was well prepared for the conversations he could encounter.

"If I was calling the huddle and they asked me questions and I didn't know answers to the questions, they're not really going to hear and focus on what I'm saying because they're going to be like, 'He doesn't even know what he's talking about so I'm not listening to him.' I made sure I was on everything. That I knew what I was talking about. The more I showed that I knew what I was talking about, the more and more respect and trust that I got."

I suspect meetings at your office are less chaotic and more orderly than calling a defensive huddle during an NFL game—or postgame interviews for that matter.

But you can apply the same approach used in both of those examples.

- **Be Prepared.** Know your stuff and have something of value to contribute.

- **Be Persistent.** Keep looking for the opening to contribute to the conversation and don't get discouraged if you get stepped on. Try, try again.

- **Be Loud (if needed).** There's probably no need to shout, but understand if you really want to be heard, sometimes you're going to have to be assertive, forceful and louder than usual. Are people going to stop and take notice when you do? Probably, and that's the point. And, it's why you need to be prepared for when you get your chance.

If you really want to make it a priority to speak up, make it a personal goal. Write it down at the same time you identify professional goals or make personal resolutions. After four seasons in the NFL, that's what Wagner did in 2016. His goals for the season not only mentioned statistical goals he wanted to reach, like the number of tackles per game or for the season, but also included the goal to be more vocal.

"When there's times that I want to say something [to my teammates] I say it," Wagner explained. "When there's something that needs to be said, I say it."

Wagner was used to saying what he needed to say in the huddle, but recognized if he wanted to step into a larger leadership role on the team, he needed to make his voice heard in other conversations.

"I talked to Coach [Pete] Carroll and I remember asking, 'how can I be a better leader?' We have so many different guys...so many leaders. That was the one thing he said to me: 'Lead the way you're supposed to lead. Find what that looks like.' Basically, just be yourself and be the best version of that. That's what I did."

That year Wagner not only became more vocal, but made his third Pro Bowl appearance, earned his second All-Pro nod, set the Seahawks franchise record for most tackles in a single season and became the first player in franchise history to record 100 or more tackles in five straight seasons. His talent and qualifications have always been a part of his game, now he's upped the ante with his communication skills.

Not Getting Challenging Assignments? Talk to Your Manager, Highlight Your Successes. Every Monday during the football season I schedule time to be interrupted. Yep, you read that right. I know my manager likes to talk about the outcome of the Seahawks game every Monday morning, so I make sure my schedule allows for it.

What does this have to do with getting challenging assignments? Because I want to encourage ongoing dialogue with the person most responsible for giving me opportunities to advance my career. I can't only talk to him during my yearly performance review and assume he knows what I'm thinking the rest of the year.

Those Monday conversations start with football, but ultimately give me an audience to talk about anything I want to bring up. For example, I could transition the conversation to talk about an idea I have for a new show, or use the time to mention I'm ready for a new challenge. This also gives me the opportunity to utilize a success statement like the ones mentioned in Chapter 2.

Building relationships with managers is just as important as building relationships with colleagues. It starts with your availability and willingness to communicate.

Being at my desk and available to talk football provides a weekly touch point, without scheduling a meeting, with the person who makes the decision on what my role is in the company, the projects I work on and if I get a pay increase. My manager has a lot on his plate, most do. It's up to me to stay on his radar and it's easier to do that when I'm sitting at my desk. Not only does he know where to find me, but he has a reason to seek me out every week during the six-month NFL season and any time there's a big football story in the off-season.

As I said in Chapter 5: sit at your desk. Make yourself available. Know what conversation topics keep you top of mind.

I know it's trendy and sometimes more convenient to work remotely. I realize not everyone has an office to go to, but you should realize this: *if it's hard for people to find you—they're only going to put in so much effort to track you down.*

You might be out of the loop without even knowing it. You might have to work twice as hard to stay on someone's radar if you're not easily available. And conversations can become more of a chore if there aren't established touch-points.

When you make it easy for people to find and talk to you, you make it easier to showcase your success and ask for a more challenging assignment.

Outside of sitting at your desk, what do you need to be available for? Happy hours? Lunch? Sticking around the office a little later than everyone else or arriving a little earlier one day a week? This is not about working longer hours. But if you're going to be stuck in traffic anyway—is there one day a week you could spend an extra hour working at your desk and being available for a conversation, instead of being stuck in a car that could be going the same speed as your career?

Feeling Left Out of Big Decisions? Initiate Conversations with Your Colleagues *Before* Your Opinion Counts. If you don't talk to your colleagues, they're not going to talk to you. It's as simple as that. It's not sexism or favoritism as much as human nature. It's also something you can influence and control.

Time spent working hard is important, but so is taking time to cultivate relationships with colleagues. Allow time for small talk during the day. It might not seem productive, but here's what happens: when you establish yourself as a good conversationalist, people want to talk to you. They'll willingly strike up a conversation. They'll get to know you, respect your opinions and perspective and be more likely to ask for your opinions on big decisions. Why? Because not only do they trust you, they're already talking to you on a regular basis.

If no one at work is coming to make small talk with you, they're also not coming to talk to you about your next career opportunity or to seek your input on a big decision.

When I need feedback on a project, I go to the colleagues I talk to most because I'm utilizing the relationships already in place.

Building relationships, being available, communicating with your manager and speaking up in meetings... it all comes back to being a good communicator and Influential Conversationalist. This is why talking is good for your career. When you become the person people want to talk to your circle of influence grows and your visibility increases along with your opportunities.

Are there still going to be challenges? Probably, but

you still control more than you think, including your willingness to communicate effectively and your ability to be heard.

Influential Conversationalist Strategy

Write It Down. What situations do you want to have more of a voice in? Is it offering to present at a meeting? Is it taking the lead on a project? Is it offering an idea during a brainstorming session? Is it highlighting a specific success during the weekly staff meeting? Write them down and assign a way to measure your success in reaching that goal.

Be Available. Decide where are you going to make yourself seen. That could mean accepting an invite to a group happy hour, joining colleagues for lunch instead of sitting at your desk, or perhaps spending *more* time at your desk when your manager is in the office.

Pick a Topic. Sports provides conversation opportunities throughout the year. You don't have to be a hardcore sports fan to make sports conversations useful in business. If fact, sports talk at work is rarely about actual sports knowledge. It's about the conversation and having a touch-point with colleagues and managers.

Sports Watch and Talk

The value of sports conversations has been mentioned a few times in this book. It might sound overly simple to say watching and talking sports can have a direct impact on your career opportunities...but something magical happens when you become the person colleagues want to talk to. You increase your visibility, open lines of communication, invite challenging conversations about opportunities you want, gain the reputation of being a good communicator, and become someone who can be counted on to carry themselves well in small talk as well as high leverage conversations.

You gotta start small to get to the big opportunities. So, here's how to use sports to your advantage.

Pick a Team: Decide what sport or team you want to talk about on a regular basis. Starting with a local team or the most popular sport in your area is a good place to begin because it's what your colleagues are already talking and hearing about most often.

Make the Time: Commit to spending (at least) 30 minutes a week building your sports knowledge base around your chosen team or sport. That's less than five minutes a day reading the sports page, following social media updates, watching highlights or tuning into a game.

Take the Initiative: Once you've got a general idea of the main storylines and talking points, start discussing them with other fans in your office. All it takes is a general comment like, "What a game last night!" to start the conversation. It's even better if you provide additional context and information by referencing a specific play or article.

> "What did you think of that Nelson Cruz home run last night?"

> "I saw there was a big feature on the Seahawks' defensive line that came out yesterday. How do you think the line is shaping up?"

You need to be the one to start the conversation if you're not already known as the person who talks about the latest sports headlines. You'll also need to initiate conversations consistently and over a period of time. Start with two conversations a week for a month.

Once colleagues get used to your interest and willingness to talk, you'll notice them starting to take the initiative, and you'll have an easy way to stay on the radar and bring conversations about sports and work to you.

A common health and fitness mantra is, "It takes 4 weeks for you to see a change, it takes 8 weeks for your friends and family, and it takes 12 weeks for everyone else." Think of your transition to an Influential Conversationalist the same way. This will not happen overnight. You need to dedicate yourself to the task. After the first few weeks, you may want to give up—but don't! If you keep at it, the shift will come.

Chapter in a Tweet…or Two

"Being a good conversationalist leads people to talk to you, know you and trust your opinions via @ TalkSportytoMe"

"If no one at work is coming to make small talk with you, they're also not coming to talk to you about your next career opportunity."

CHAPTER 9

What's Left to Say?

I was a voracious reader as a kid. From time to time, I remember jumping ahead to the final pages of the story to see if the ending was as good as I thought. If so, I'd try to read even faster to get to the good stuff.

If you've jumped ahead in this book, I made sure to include some of the good stuff. Hopefully it will encourage you to go back and dig into the other chapters.

The things left to say are actual words and phrases an Influential Conversationalist should use often. They'll put you in positions to grow and to develop skills that get you noticed and make you more interesting for other people to talk to. They'll open doors that give you visibility with decision makers and provide perspectives leaders seek out.

These conversations determine the plotline for the rest of your story, which I wouldn't draw any conclusions about now. Remember Chapter 6, you're the hero of your own story. You're not at the end yet and there's no way to predict just how far you'll go.

Here are things you as an Influential Conversationalists need to be able to say:

"I'll Get Better."

You're going to make mistakes, but you don't have to (and shouldn't be trying to) figure it out on your own. You need to be humble enough to know you're not perfect, and you need to be coachable enough to handle feedback and learn from constructive criticism. It's okay to take a job you'll grow into. It's not okay to be stubborn, ornery or defiant about how you're approaching that job.

"If you come into anything and you're just trying to lead right out of the gate and be the boss out of the gate, that doesn't always sit too well," Mariners third baseman Kyle Seager says. "You have to earn people's respect. You've got to work through it. And to do that you have to be open and you have to be able to listen."

You also need to realize that as comfortable as you might get doing a job, the three most dangerous words according to Seahawks linebacker K.J. Wright are, "I've got it," because it signals you're not as hungry to learn or improve.

"You've always got to strive to be your best," Wright said. "If you think something is simple to you, find ways to make it even more simple. If covering receivers is easy, find ways to cover them and intercept the ball. You're always striving to be better—once you say, 'I've got it,' that's when complacency starts to set in and that's when you lose focus of what you need to be working on."

"Nice Win!"

Define success. Know what constitutes a win and celebrate. Sports fans celebrate team wins and the accomplishments of their favorite athletes. They often fail to apply that same awareness or enthusiasm in celebrating their own accomplishments.

As an Influential Conversationalist, people are going to be looking at how you handle success. Find a way to acknowledge your own wins so you can encourage others to not only do the same, but be inspired to find even more success.

"The first thing is setting goals and knowing what you want to accomplish as an individual, as a team, as a group," Arizona Diamondbacks catcher, Chris Iannetta suggests. "Anytime you reach one of those milestones, celebrate it and be proud of it. Winning isn't easy. There are people failing at the thing you just accomplished. Take some time to acknowledge it."

"Everyone enjoys getting patted on the back," Mariners utility player Shawn O'Malley agreed. "Knowing when you've done a good job...I think it makes you strive for something more than what you just did. It feels like business is a team effort, so I think when you applaud your team on their success they'll strive to do better. They want to do more for each other. It's a snowball effect of good things."

"It Doesn't Matter."

This is not meant as a snarky retort or huffy comment. It's an internal response when outsiders want to minimize your success. It happens all the time in sports. Fans, commentators and even opponents weigh in on whether a player is having a good or a bad year. It's another reason why knowing what success looks like is important—because too many outside factors can detract from your accomplishments.

"You never want to feel like you need someone else to validate your success, or that you need accolades to validate your success," Seahawks linebacker Bobby Wagner said, "We talk about that all the time [in the locker room]. That's being talked about way, way, before the season starts: is not letting something else be the foundation of your success."

"I'm Going to Get the Job Done."

You're going to run into doubters at some point during your career. Someone is going to challenge if you have the skills it takes or whether you're up for the job. Don't get frustrated. There are likely to be skeptics...until you prove them wrong. You don't have to be better than everyone else, but you do have to be confident enough to show them what you've got. It's even more important if the doubter is you. (If you have issues with negative self-talk, see Chapter 6.)

"Confidence has a lot to do with it, because it's belief

in yourself," said Seahawks cornerback Richard Sherman. "It's belief that it's not as much about the other person, and more about yourself. It's not as much about their execution as it is my execution. There are people who are faster, bigger, stronger—and when you realize: if my technique is flawless and I play the way I'm supposed to play it won't matter what he does, who he is or what he's capable of, I'll be able to get through it."

"There are times in baseball where you doubt yourself," O'Malley admitted. "You don't think you're better than somebody but mentally when you dial in and say, 'I'm going to get the job done,' you'll be surprised at the mental power you have over something like that. You don't have to control everything, but you give yourself a better fighting chance."

"I think all of us would admit that deep down we do lack confidence at times and experience it during games," Seahawks wide receiver Doug Baldwin said. "I have to block out the negative thoughts that my mind creates. In terms of thinking, 'What happens if the defensive back gets his hands on you? What happens if you drop the ball?' Those negative things can spiral out of control."

Baldwin recalled a specific example of letting negative thoughts impact his play. "It was a game against Tampa Bay and I had two or three drops in the first quarter, and a coach comes up to me on the sideline and asks if I'm alright then says, 'Wake up!'"

Instead of giving in to the doubts and the "what if's"

he coached himself up and talked his way back into a more confident state of mind.

"It was basically positive self-talk and remembering all the training, all the preparation that I'd put in up to that point to realize I was good enough in that moment. And I would continue to be good enough as long as I continued to have that positive mindset."

Baldwin went on to score a touchdown and finished the game as the team's leading receiver.

"Yes, I'd Be Happy to do That."

That's an easy thing to say when you've been asked to do something you wanted to do. You need to be able to say it with sincerity, even when it's a part of the job you hate or it's something you have no interest in doing. Everyone wants to do the cool jobs. You don't stand out if you're doing the fun stuff. You stand out when you cheerfully do the job no one else wanted to do, or when you recognize there's something that isn't being done and take the initiative to do it on your own. That's how leaders lead.

Everyone, even athletes, have had jobs we didn't like or didn't see the long-term value in at the time. Have you ever looked back and realized how much the worst jobs or the worst part of your job prepared you for what you're doing now?

"Picking weeds out of the garden," Kyle Seager said of his worst job as a kid. "We grew up on a little farm, and in the summer we wanted to go to the pool. We wanted to hang out with our friends. We couldn't do that until we had picked the weeds—or picking beans was the worst. You look back on it and it's a life lesson that I hope to instill in my son. You get that work ethic. If you do what you're supposed to be doing and you get your job done, you can go out and have fun and do what you want to do. But there's work that needs to be done."

"When I was a kid, probably 10 years old, my grandad was a carpenter and he always took me and my cousins with him to work in the summer time," K.J. Wright recalled. "Of course, we had to wake up early, do all the dirty work. It taught me a lot. It taught me how to work hard. It taught me to wake up early. And it taught me about listening, because he used to tell me something and if I messed up, he would get on me."

Shawn O'Malley sees a direct correlation between the time he spent working at a winery during fall harvest and the way he approaches his job as a baseball player. "I think being on time, doing my job right, taking pride in whatever it is," O'Malley said. "If I'm cleaning buckets or transferring wine to tanks, or coming up to bat in the 9th inning with the game winning run on second base. I think it's one of those things you take pride in because your name is on it at the end of the day, and you want to be the most ready to do the best job you can every day."

The Rest of the Story

The motivation behind why you read the book will likely dictate how much you get out of it. When you apply the strategies outlined here try to view them, not just as a how-to guide for workplace conversations, but as a way to view every conversation as a potential opportunity.

That's why I wrote the book. I wanted to give you tools that empowered you to champion yourself, create more opportunities and step into leadership roles without needing someone to give you permission or a title. I wanted to give you something to say when you faced opposition, felt defeated and lost the ability to see your own brilliance.

I wanted to give you the same techniques that got me to where I am in my career. I wanted to teach you what to say because based on what I was told, I never should have succeeded:

- I was told women don't belong in sports.

- I was told by a former manager in my first television job that I was hired to wear short skirts and open doors, not to think or contribute to conversations.

- I was told I belonged in the kitchen where I could cook and clean, not on the football field where I could officiate.

- I was told I wasn't pretty enough for TV.

- I was told I was just a pretty face, and full of shit.

Every time someone told me something that sounded like, "No" I talked my way into a new opportunity. I sought out conversations with influencers who could give me a chance. I found ways to show up over and over again. I rehearsed conversations I had with decision makers. I built relationships and I stayed on the radar. I was able to do all of this because I am an Influential Conversationalist. Good communication skills open doors and make a difference.

Oh, there's one more thing I was told, by my mother who told me I shouldn't take a picture flipping off the camera with my Super Bowl ring.

I usually listen to my mother, but after all the things I've been told, I say that picture Finally Underscores my accomplishments.

Influential Conversationalist Strategy

Just do it. You've got enough strategies at this point to make these conversations easier. Commit to doing it.

Pick two strategies mentioned in the book and identify two situations to put them into practice this week. Make a note on your calendar. Set an alarm. Leave a sticky note on your computer. Whatever is needed for you to act. Don't wait to take steps toward becoming an Influential Conversationalist.

Sports Watch and Talk

When you're watching a game or a sportscast you're bound to hear a broadcaster or reporter flub a line, recover and continue their thought. Professional communicators don't always say the right thing, or say what they're trying to say perfectly.

You're not always going to say the right thing or even know what the right thing is to say. Don't give up. Keep going. There are too many opportunities out there for you to avoid conversations or ignore the type of communication that leads to a big break.

You've got this. Start talking.

Chapter in a Tweet...or Two

"Be coachable. It's okay to take a job you'll grow into. It's not okay to be stubborn or defiant about how you're approaching that job."

"You stand out when you cheerfully do the job or task no one else wanted to do. That's how leaders lead according to @JenTalksSports"

The No-Stress Way to Build Rapport

The first day of baseball's Spring Training and football Training Camp bring the same mix of emotions for me. I'm excited to start the season, anxious to see colleagues I haven't talked to since the previous season, and nervous about walking into the clubhouse or locker room for the first time. Seeing familiar faces is easy. It's meeting all the new additions that can make me apprehensive. I'm not shy about meeting new people, but in those situations I'm hyper-aware of the importance of making a good impression and building a relationship. I know my success for the next six months depends in part on their willingness to talk to me. That's why those initial trips into the locker room feel a bit more daunting.

Those relationships start by building rapport. During my conversations with athletes through the years, I've learned rapport is built in little ways. My father demonstrated to me how it's the same in business. As a

CEO, anyone calling to talk to him had to get past his assistant. Vendors or sales people would call saying they were old friends of my father. His assistant was smart, sharp as a tack and knew better, but she would pass the message along.

If my father had the opportunity, he would take the call. His opening line sounded similar every time, "I understand we're good friends and have known each other for years." My father would say. The sales person would inevitably respond, "Well, no, I just said that to get past your assistant." To which my father would respond. "So, you lied. Why would I do business with you?" The sales person would start fumbling around. And my father would cut to the chase and say, "You lied to my assistant to get to me, why would I trust that you wouldn't lie to me?"

And then hang up.

He did the same thing when sales people called and asked for sixty seconds of his time and couldn't finish their pitch in sixty seconds. To him, it was another form of lying. (And a good way to prove his point to people who thought they were scamming the system.)

Here's the thing about rapport, on the surface, it seems elusive. In practice, it's doing what you say you're going to do time after time (which builds the relationship that leads to business transactions).

Follow these steps to take the stress out of building rapport:

Be Direct and Make the Introduction. It's the hardest and the easiest step to make. Walking up, saying "Hi" and introducing yourself isn't always comfortable, but it sure beats the alternative of becoming known as a weirdo. If I stand in the locker room without talking to anyone, it raises questions as to why I'm there in the first place. I've had several players over the years observe that behavior in other media members and ask me why the guy in the tan pants or the gal in a black jacket are just standing there when the people they need to talk to are sitting right in front of them. Meanwhile, "guy-in-tan-pants" and "girl-in-black-jacket" have no idea they've even made an impression (much less a potentially poor impression). Go up and introduce yourself.

Realize the Expectation is Already Set. When I'm in a locker room, guys expect me to ask for an interview. When I walk up to them after the game, it's not to get a recommendation on where to go to dinner—it's actually work related and task oriented.

In most cases, the expectations are set for many of your workplace conversations too. When you make an introduction, there's an assumption a business conversation will follow. Hopefully, knowing this will alleviate some of the stress and fear you might have around these interactions so you can get out of your own head and have the conversations you need to have.

Be Clear on Your Intent. There's a reason you engaged in the conversation in the first place. Don't keep it a secret. Express your intent or desired outcome. Here's how that might sound in a locker room:

> "Hey Brandon, I'm Jen Mueller. I work on the Seahawks broadcast doing pre- and postgame interviews. At some point, I'm going to ask you for a postgame interview. Just wanted to introduce myself."

> "Hi Sam, nice to meet you, congrats on your call up. I work on the Mariners television broadcast. Could I get a two-minute interview with you on camera before the game?"

Two different scenarios, two different asks—but both very clear. And in both examples, it removes the guessing-game distraction. I don't want a player to guess what the "ask" is going to be, or create any confusion over next steps. The quicker you communicate this information, the more productive the conversation becomes. Don't think you're dropping hints by making general statements and hoping someone picks up on the messages you're sending telepathically. For example, if you want your colleague to offer to find a venue for the Christmas party, don't casually say, "The committee working on the company Christmas party meets next week." And expect him to respond with, "Oh great, I'd love to help pick the venue."

Cut to the chase and be clear with your intent. "The committee working on the Christmas party meets next week. You mentioned a few ideas for the venue. Would you be willing to reach out to three venues about pricing and availability?"

Make the "Real" Ask. In other words, don't ask for one thing only to make the "real" ask after you've gotten a commitment. For example, don't ask for a get-to-know-you coffee meeting, if what you really wanted was an introduction to the CEO. A "bait and switch" approach isn't going to work or help you to build rapport. If the person isn't interested or on board with your real ask, a cup of coffee isn't going to change that. Suckering someone into one thing does not increase the likelihood they'll say yes to another thing.

Timing is Everything. As in, if I ask for a two-minute interview, guess how long that interview lasts? Two minutes. If I say I have three questions for a player. How many questions do I ask? You guessed it—exactly three. It sounds simplistic, but it's a way to build trust. If I ask for two minutes of your time and then talk for 20, how likely are you to believe me the next time when I tell you something is just going to take two minutes? If I know it's going to take 20 minutes I need to ask for 20 minutes. Be honest and stick to your word.

Be Realistic. Don't believe the people who say, "It doesn't hurt to ask." Making an unrealistic ask can damage the rapport you're trying to build, and demonstrate a lack of self-awareness. If you're at a networking event and you meet the CEO of a Fortune 100 company, asking for a follow up lunch meeting is a long shot that shows you're unaware of the time constraints in an executive's schedule. Unless you're also an executive or hold a comparable status, asking for a 15-minute phone call would be a more realistic and appropriate first step.

Bringing It All Together

Building rapport is at the core of being an Influential Conversationalist. That can seem like a broad concept, but that is why this list is so useful. It takes the stress out of building rapport because it's simple. And the good news is, there are so many opportunities to utilize this approach in daily interactions (you'll be amazed once you start noticing them). Before you know it you'll be building rapport all over the place. You don't have to go out of your way, you just need the discipline to stick to your word. And remember, every conversation has the potential to impact your future opportunities.

Becoming an Influential Conversationalist will open doors you never thought possible, and can absolutely change your life. If you use the tips in this book consistently every day (no one and done here!) you will see positive changes in yourself and your relationships. Are you ready to be an Influential Conversationalist?

Chapter in a Tweet...or Two

"There are too many opportunities out there for you to avoid conversations. Start talking and become an Influential Conversationalist."

ABOUT THE AUTHOR

Jen Mueller pursued a career in sports broadcasting after repeated comments of "talks too much" from teachers and family members. She currently serves as the sideline radio reporter for the Seattle Seahawks and is a member of the Seattle Mariners television broadcast on ROOT SPORTS. In addition to her on-air work, Jen is an Emmy-award winning producer for her work on Mariners All Access and a former high school football official.

Jen launched Talk Sporty to Me in 2009 and teaches corporate clients how to make sports conversations useful in business. Jen is a talented and dynamic speaker with unique content and personal stories from inside professional locker rooms. She is also the author of "Talk Sporty to Me: Thinking Outside the Box Scores" published in 2015.

Jen graduated from Southern Methodist University in 2000 with degrees in broadcasting journalism and public policy. She currently lives in the Seattle area with her husband Paul.

To hire Jen to speak at your conference or event please email: Jen@TalkSportytoMe.com